Objectives for Instruction and Evaluation

Second Edition

Donald J. Cegala
Ohio State University

Kittie W. Watson
Tulane University

Larry L. Barker
Auburn University

David T. Miles
Southern Illinois University

Allyn and Bacon, Inc.
Boston   London   Sydney   Toronto

Portions of this book first appeared in *Behavioral Objectives and Instruction*, copyright © 1970 by Allyn and Bacon, Inc.

Library of Congress Cataloging in Publication Data
Main entry under title:

Objectives for instruction and evaluation.

Bibliography: p.
Includes index.
1. Teaching. 2. Education—Aims and objectives.
3. Curriculum evaluation. 4. Education—United States. I. Kibler, Robert J., 1934–June 28, 1978
LB1025.2.02 1981   371.1'02   80-19694
ISBN 0-205-07154-6
ISBN 0-205-07174-0 (pbk.)

Printed in the United States of America.

Contents

Preface

Educational objectives have been examined and discussed throughout the history of education. More recently, the work in programmed learning and instructional technology has heightened interest in the specification of precise educational objectives. Numerous books and journal articles have appeared in the literature in response to this interest in specifying precise instructional goals. This book represents an effort to identify important functions that instructional objectives can serve in improving instruction. We hope the book will contribute to the continuing effort to improve the quality and efficiency of instruction by shaping favorable attitudes toward the use of instructional objectives, by informing individuals about the nature and characteristics of objectives, and by helping educators to write objectives. We feel that teachers, administrators, curriculum planners. members of school boards, and researchers will find this book useful.

Approximately seven years have lapsed since the appearance of the first edition of *Objectives for Instruction and Evaluation*. During that time several important developments have surfaced in all facets of our educational system. Although the second edition does address many of the relevant issues that have appeared since the first edition, this book is still intended to be a supplementary text. However, we have expanded this edition of the book by:

Updating sources and research findings on instructional objectives.

Including material on needs assessment and its relationship to the use of instructional objectives.

Including a new chapter on task analysis and behavior domains.

Extending the discussion of alternative instructional strategies.

In addition to incorporating these new aspects, the book maintains its original contributions:

It provides in a single volume material relative to instructional objectives gleaned from a variety of sources.

It presents a classroom-tested model of instruction that illustrates the relationships of instructional objectives to the instruction-learning process.

It analyzes in detail the elements contained in objectives that are required to plan instruction.

It describes procedures for matching objectives and evaluation strategies.

It examines the relationship between instructional objectives, criterion-referenced evaluation, and mastery learning.

The authors express their sincere appreciation to all of the individuals who graciously permitted us to reprint their materials and to all of the publishers and institutions who granted us permission to reproduce copyrighted materials. We also would like to express our deepest sadness for the untimely death of our respected and loved colleague and friend, Robert J. Kibler. It was his commitment to excellence and his concern for students that initially brought together the ideas for this book. We will be forever indebted to him for his insights and guidance, and we dedicate this edition of the book to his memory.

D. J. C.
K. W. W.
L. L. B.
D. T. M.

1

Instructional Objectives and the Instructional Process

After completing this chapter, the learner should be able to:

1. Define the term *instructional objective*;
2. List ten reasons for using instructional objectives in education;
3. Describe the current status of empirical research on instructional objectives;
4. Identify three methodological weaknesses characterizing empirical research on instructional objectives that may account for inconsistent research findings;
5. Identify fourteen key points of controversy over the use of instructional objectives;
6. List and explain eight points of controversy in the use of objective-based programs;
7. Identify three values that instructional objectives have for students;
8. Identify two values that instructional objectives have for teachers;
9. Describe how instructional objectives can aid administrators;
10. Describe how instructional objectives can aid administrators in their dealings with school boards and parents.

In this chapter we present a general rationale for using instructional objectives. Reasons for using instructional objectives are examined from three perspectives: a *rational* (or intuitive) perspective, an *empirical* perspective, and a *functional* perspective.

The Rationale for Instructional Objectives and Their Use

Since the major focus of this book is on the nature and use of instructional objectives, it will be helpful to clarify at the outset what we mean by the term *instructional objective*. Instructional objectives are statements that describe what students will be able to do after completing a prescribed unit of instruction. Other terms that have been used to describe these types of objectives (i.e., instructional) are *behavioral objectives* and *performance goals*. The terms *behavioral* and *performance* often are used to describe objectives of the nature we will examine because the objectives inform students what behaviors or performances (e.g., write an essay, draw a diagram, construct a model) they are expected to achieve to demonstrate that they have learned what is required of them.

Since Chapter 3 is devoted to a detailed examination of instructional objectives, we will not take time here to describe the characteristics and components of instructional objectives. However, an example of an instructional objective is given to establish an understanding of the term. Below are two objectives; the first is *not* an instructional objective, while the second one is (additional sample objectives are provided in Appendix A):

1. The student will know what factors gave rise to the Industrial Revolution.
2. The student will list and describe in writing at least three factors that gave rise to the Industrial Revolution.

The second objective informs the student what to *do* (i.e., list and describe in writing at least three factors that gave rise to the Industrial Revolution) to demonstrate that learning has occurred. The first objective lacks specificity; it does not indicate *how* the student is to demonstrate knowledge and to what extent he/she is to know the required information. Additional distinguishing characteristics of instructional objectives will be presented and discussed later. At this time, it is important to consider reasons for using instructional objectives.

Rational Basis for Using Instructional Objectives

Instructional objectives are used at all levels of education (e.g., elementary, secondary, and higher education). One reason for the use of instructional objectives is that they are consistent with the concept of accountability (the balancing of money spent for education to amount of student learning). Accountability in education is rapidly gaining acceptance from both the public and the federal government. The publicity given the Texarkana program (Elam, 1970) and others like it has stimulated the belief that application of accountability concepts to public education is a "concrete practical activity." Hopefully, instructional objectives will be used to confront some of the most critical educational dilemmas, including the reestablishment of confidence in the educational system at all levels (Lessinger, 1970; Niedermeyer and Sullivan, 1977).

Some educators perceive accountability as a threat to the educational process. Many of these educators who have negative attitudes about accountability have also become negative about instructional objectives. Apparently, their negative attitudes are based on the misconception that using instructional objectives leads to accountability in education. The use of instructional objectives is consistent with accountability, but national and local economic considerations, rather than the mere use of instructional objectives are what ultimately lead to accountability-based educational systems.

Few comforting words can be said to those teachers who view accountability-based educational systems as a threat. However, if accountability-based educational systems do become the norm, experience in the use of instructional objectives will enable teachers to adapt to the system more easily. To achieve the balance between spending and student learning that accountability demands, the individual teacher or school system must be able to demonstrate that students have learned as a result of their instruction. Accordingly, educational accountability can be implemented successfully only if educational goals or objectives are precisely identified and stated before the instructional program begins and if some reliable measure of effectiveness of instruction in implementing these goals is devised.

The use of instructional objectives allows teachers to state specific instructional goals to immediate supervisors and school boards. Instructional objectives also aid teachers in assessing student attainment of the specified goals (as we shall see in Chapter 7). While the issue of accountability is one of the most compelling reasons for using instructional objectives, there are additional reasons for their use in the educational process (Kibler and Barker, 1970; Kibler, Barker, and Cegala, 1970b). Among the additional reasons for using instructional objectives are the following:

1. Because instructional objectives specify clearly to students what is to be learned and how they are to demonstrate learning (including a statement of the criteria to be used in evaluating learners' performance), it seems reasonable to argue that students are spared the frustration and time-consuming effort of trying to guess what the teacher expects of them. Moreover, it appears logical that students will learn more easily if they are told what they are expected to learn and how they will be expected to demonstrate that learning has occurred.
2. Curriculum planners are better able to arrange sequences of courses or units of instruction when given clearly specified objectives. Knowledge of the necessary prerequisite and terminal skills pertinent to various courses should eliminate unnecessary course overlap and help to identify gaps between courses.
3. Students and their advisors are able to plan their course programs more effectively when they can read course descriptions that include instructional objectives.
4. Clear instructional objectives enable teachers to tell other teachers specifically what they teach. Stating that "Students learn to name each state in the United States and its capital" communicates considerably more than simply stating, "United States geography is taught."
5. Teachers and administrators can determine the level of objectives students will be able to achieve in terms of the three taxonomic classifications to be discussed in Chapter 4. For example, in the cognitive domain, objectives can be classified as knowledge, comprehension, application, analysis, synthesis, and evaluation, thereby avoiding undue emphasis on a certain level of objectives.
6. Clearly defined goals help teachers in designing instructional experiences and evaluating the effectiveness of such experiences according to whether the goals are achieved.

7. Gagné (1965a) has pointed out the need for student evaluation in educational programs. It is important for the teacher to be able to determine the student's capabilities at any time during an instructional program. When instructional objectives are specified, it is possible for the teacher to determine the student's present level of mastery for a prescribed objective at any time. In addition, specific instructional objectives help teachers to identify students who have acquired, prior to instruction, the level of excellence required for successful performance on a given objective. Instructional objectives also help identify students who lack the prerequisites to master the prescribed objectives successfully.

8. Instructional objectives include a performance standard that represents a minimal level of performance to be sought by all, or most, students. Therefore, most students in a given class can be expected to master successfully the behavior specified in an objective. This idea may seem startling—that most students in a class can succeed. However, such outstanding psychologists as Bloom (1968) and Carroll (1963) have argued that most students can achieve mastery if they will (and are permitted to) devote enough time to the learning task and if appropriate instruction is provided.

9. Performance standards help teachers determine the adequacy of their instructional program. If students do not master objectives efficiently as a result of a given instructional program, various changes may be required in the program, in the objectives, or in other elements of the instructional process.

Empirical Basis for Using Instructional Objectives

Several reasons for using instructional objectives have already been mentioned; however, we have not given empirical data for their support. Early research studying the use of instructional objectives found inconsistencies and little conclusive evidence concerning the relationship between learning success and the use of instructional objectives. These inconsistencies led many educators to be skeptical of the use of instructional objectives. However, much of the early research on the use of instructional objectives was characterized by significant methodological weaknesses.

Three methodological concerns seem particularly worthy of comment here. First, methods of operationalizing instructional objectives are not standard across experimental studies.

Researchers often do not report examples of instructional objectives used in the studies. For this reason, it is difficult, if not impossible, to determine the worth of the objectives used.

Second, very few researchers have provided subjects with instruction in the use of objectives prior to experimental treatment conditions. Since instructional objectives are new to most students, prior training in the use of objectives may be an important factor in determining how objectives affect learning (Tiemann, 1968; Boardman, 1970; Brown, 1970; Jenkins and Deno, 1971; Tobias and Duchastel, 1972; Bassett, 1973). In addition, experiences in using instructional objectives in our classes also support this notion. Appendix B contains a programmed text designed to teach students how to use instructional objectives. The reader may find this program useful in teaching students how to benefit maximally from instructional objectives.

_____Branching Option One_____

At this point in the text, the reader has the option of turning to additional material in Appendix B. Appendix B is designed to teach you how to use instructional objectives. You may read the material at this point for purposes of clarity, or you may choose to complete the reading of this section and turn to the Appendix at a later time.

Third, few researchers have provided teachers with training in the use of instructional objectives. Consequently, it is difficult to determine if objectives were used appropriately in many of the reported studies. Three suggestions may improve research investigating the use of instructional objectives in the classroom (Kibler, Bassett, and Byers, 1977). First, most research measured lower-order behaviors in learning. Additional studies need to include instructional objectives and related measures that examine various levels of learning. Second, the instructional objectives in previous studies were classified in the cognitive domain. Objectives should be included in the affective and psychomotor domains as well. Third, future research needs to give more attention to the reliability and validity of the data. It is impossible for educators to place confidence in research results without verification of the results.

While problems with earlier research on the use of instructional objectives precluded a clear empirical assessment of their effectiveness on learning, more recent research findings are less ambiguous. For example, reviews on incidental and intentional learning (Duchastel and Merrill, 1973) and on mastery learning (Block, 1971; Block and Anderson, 1975) suggest that students are more likely to achieve clearly stated goals and objectives than ambiguous or unknown ones. The majority of research confirms the view that students who know specific instructional objectives achieve more than students unaware of instructional objectives (Dawley and Dawley, 1974; Duchastel and Brown, 1975; Hauck and Thomas, 1972; Houston and Warner, 1977; Kibler, Bassett, and Byers, 1977; Morse and Tellman, 1972; Rothkopf and Kaplan, 1972; Wolk, 1973). In conformity with research findings, many textbook series now include instructional objectives because of their usefulness (Ohrtman, 1976).

Current research findings support the use of instructional objectives to enhance learning. Along with an empirical basis, we have presented several logical reasons for using instructional objectives. Even so, there are a number of educators who perceive equally logical reasons for not using instructional objectives (Hausdorf, 1965; Eisner, 1967; Ebel, 1970; Macdonald and Walfron, 1970). The controversy among educators has generated a number of heated discussions regarding the importance and use of objectives in the classroom.

Functional Basis for Using Instructional Objectives

Many of the controversies about instructional objectives stem either from differing philosophical views about the nature of education or from questions about how instructional objectives are applied to certain areas of education, such as the fine arts and humanities. In essence, the controversy often focuses on differing viewpoints about how instructional objectives function in an educational system. W. James Popham has written an insightful paper dealing with several arguments that have been presented in opposition to instructional objectives. Dr. Popham's paper is reproduced below as an introduction to some of the key points of controversy over their use.

Probing the Validity of Arguments Against Behavioral Goals*

W. James Popham
University of California, Los Angeles
Southwest Regional Laboratory
for Educational Research and Development

Within the last few years a rather intense debate has developed in the field of curriculum and instruction regarding the merits of stating instructional objectives in terms of measurable behaviors. Because I am thoroughly committed, both rationally and viscerally, to the proposition that instructional goals should be stated behaviorally, I view this debate with some ambivalence. On the one hand, it is probably desirable to have a dialogue of this sort among specialists in our field. We get to know each other better—between attacks. We test the respective worth of opposing positions. We can have hopefully stimulating symposia such as this one. Yet, as a partisan in the controversy, I would prefer unanimous support of the position to which I subscribe. You see, the other people are wrong. Adhering to a philosophic tenet that error is evil, I hate to see my friends wallowing in sin.

Moreover, their particular form of sin is more dangerous than some of the time-honored perversions of civilized societies. For example, it will probably harm more people than the most exotic forms of pornography. I believe that those who discourage educators from precisely explicating their instructional objectives are often permitting, if not promoting, the same kind of unclear thinking that has led in part to the generally abysmal quality of instruction in this country.

In the remainder of this paper I shall examine eleven reasons given by my colleagues in opposition to objectives stated in terms of measurable learner behaviors. I believe each of these reasons is, for the most part, invalid. There may be minor elements of truth in some; after all, the most vile pornographer must occasionally use a few clean words. In essence, however, none of these reasons should be considered

---

*This paper was presented at the annual American Educational Research Association meeting, Chicago, February 7-10, 1968. The authors are indebted to Dr. Popham for granting permission to publish the paper in this volume.

strong enough to deter educators from specifying all of their instructional goals in the precise form advocated by the "good guys" in this argument.

I shall not attempt to develop any arguments in favor of precisely stated goals, for these are treated elsewhere.* My only concern will be with the dubious validity of each of the following reasons.†

Reason one: Trivial learner behaviors are the easiest to operationalize, hence the really important outcomes of education will be underemphasized.

This particular objection to the use of precise goals is frequently voiced by educators who have recently become acquainted with the procedures for stating explicit, behavioral objectives. Since even behavioral objectives enthusiasts admit that the easiest kinds of pupil behaviors to operationalize are usually the most pedestrian, it is not surprising to find so many examples of behavioral objectives which deal with the picayune. In spite of its overall beneficial influence, the programmed booklet by Robert Mager (1962) dealing with the preparation of instructional objectives has probably suggested to many that precise objectives are usually trivial. Almost all of Mager's examples deal with cognitive behaviors which, according to Bloom's taxonomy, would be identified at the very lowest level.

Contrary to the objection raised in reason one, however, the truth is that explicit objectives make it far *easier* for educators to attend to *important* instructional outcomes. To illustrate, if you were to ask a social science teacher what his objectives were for his government class and he responded as follows, "I want to make my students better citizens so that they can function effectively in our nation's dynamic democracy," you would probably find little reason to fault him. His objective sounds so profound and eminently worthwhile that few could criticize it. Yet, beneath such facades of profundity, many teachers really are aiming at extremely trivial kinds of

---

*W. James Popham, *Educational Objectives.* Los Angeles: Vimcet Associates, 1966; W. James Popham, *Selecting Appropriate Educational Objectives.* Los Angeles: Vimcet Associates, 1967.
†Many of the following remarks are adapted from a symposium presentation at the 19th Annual Conference on Educational Research, California Advisory Council on Educational Research, San Diego, November 16, 1967.

pupil behavior changes. How often, for example, do we find "good citizenship" measured by a trifling true-false test. Now if we'd asked for the teacher's objectives in operational terms and had discovered that, indeed, all the teacher was attempting to do was promote the learner's achievement on a true-false test, we might have rejected the aim as being unimportant. But this is possible *only* with the precision of explicitly stated goals.

In other words, there is the danger that because of their ready translation to operational statements, teachers will tend to identify too many trivial behaviors as goals. But the very fact that we can make these behaviors explicit permits the teacher and his colleagues to scrutinize them carefully and thus eliminate them as unworthy of our educational efforts. Instead of encouraging unimportant outcomes in education, the use of explicit instructional objectives makes it possible to identify and reject those objectives which are unimportant.

Reason two: Prespecification of explicit goals prevents the teacher from taking advantage of instructional opportunities unexpectedly occurring in the classroom.

When one specifies explicit *ends* for an instructional program there is no necessary implication that the *means* to achieve those ends are also specified. Serendipity in the classroom is always welcome but, and here is the important point, *it should always be justified in terms of its contribution to the learner's attainment of worthwhile objectives.* Too often teachers may believe they are capitalizing on unexpected instructional opportunities in the classroom, whereas measurement of pupil growth toward any defensible criterion would demonstrate that what has happened is merely ephemeral entertainment for the pupils, temporary diversion, or some other irrelevant classroom event.

Prespecification of explicit goals does not prevent the teacher from taking advantage of unexpectedly occurring instructional opportunities in the classroom; it only tends to make the teacher justify these spontaneous learning activities in terms of worthwhile instructional ends. There are undoubtedly gifted teachers who can capitalize magnificently on the most unexpected classroom events. These teachers should not be restricted from doing so. But the teacher who prefers to probe instructional periphery, just for the sake of its spontaneity, should be deterred by the prespecification of explicit goals.

Reason three: Besides pupil behavior changes, there are other types of educational outcomes which are important, such as changes in parental attitudes, the professional staff, community values, etc.

There are undoubtedly some fairly strong philosophic considerations associated with this particular reason. It seems reasonable that there are desirable changes to be made in our society which might be undertaken by the schools. Certainly, we would like to bring about desirable modifications in such realms as the attitudes of parents. But as a number of educational philosophers have reminded us, the schools cannot be all things to all segments of society. It seems that the primary responsibility of the schools should be to educate effectively the youth of the society. And to the extent that this is so, all modifications of parental attitudes, professional staff attitudes, etc., should be weighed in terms of a later measurable impact on the learner himself. For example, the school administrator who tells us that he wishes to bring about new kinds of attitudes on the part of his teachers should ultimately have to demonstrate that these modified attitudes result in some kind of desirable learner changes. To stop at merely modifying the behavior of teachers, without demonstrating further effects upon the learner, would be insufficient.

So while we can see that there are other types of important social outcomes to bring about, it seems that the school's primary responsibility is to its pupils. Hence, all modifications in personnel or external agencies should be justified in terms of their contribution toward the promotion of desired pupil behavior changes.

Reason four: Measurability implies behavior which can be objectively, mechanistically measured, hence there must be something dehumanizing about the approach.

This fourth reason is drawn from a long history of resistance to measurement on the grounds that it must, of necessity, reduce human learners to quantifiable bits of data. This resistance probably is most strong regarding earlier forms of measurement which were almost exclusively examination-based, and were frequently multiple-choice test measures at that. But a broadened conception of evaluation suggests that there are diverse and extremely sophisticated ways of securing qualitative as well as quantitative indices of learner performance.

One is constantly amazed to note the incredible agreement among a group of judges assigned to evaluate the complicated gyrations of skilled springboard divers in the televised reports of national aquatic championships. One of these athletes will perform an exotic, twisting dive and a few seconds after he has hit the water five or more judges raise cards reflecting their independent evaluations which can range from 0 to 10. The five ratings very frequently run as follows: 7.8, 7.6, 7.7, 7.8, and 7.5. The possibility of reliably judging something as qualitatively complicated as a springboard dive does suggest that our measurement procedures do not have to be based on a theory of reductionism. It is currently possible to assess many complicated human behaviors in a refined fashion. Developmental work is underway in those areas where we now must rely on primitive measures.

Reason five: It is somehow undemocratic to plan in advance precisely how the learner should behave after instruction.
        This particular reason was raised a few years ago in a professional journal (Arnstine, 1964) suggesting that the programmed instruction movement was basically undemocratic because it spelled out in advance how the learner was supposed to behave after instruction. A brilliant refutation (Komisar and McClellan, 1965) appeared several months later in which the rebutting authors responded that instruction is by its very nature undemocratic and to imply that freewheeling democracy is always present in the classroom would be untruthful. Teachers generally have an idea of how they wish learners to behave, and they promote these goals with more or less efficiency. Society knows what it wants its young to become, perhaps not with the precision that we would desire, but certainly in general. And if the schools were allowing students to "democratically" deviate from societally-mandated goals, one can be sure that the institutions would cease to receive society's approbation and support.

Reason six: That isn't really the way teaching is; teachers rarely specify their goals in terms of measurable learner behaviors; so let's set realistic expectations of teachers.
        Jackson (1966) recently offered this argument. He observed that teachers just don't specify their objectives in terms of measurable learner behavior and implied that, since this is

the way the real world is, we ought to recognize it and live with it. Perhaps.

There is obviously a difference between identifying the status quo and applauding it. Most of us would readily concede that few teachers specify their instructional aims in terms of measurable learner behavior, *but they ought to.* What we have to do is to mount a widespread campaign to modify this aspect of teacher behavior. Instructors must begin to identify their instructional intentions in terms of measurable learner behaviors. The way teaching really is at the moment just isn't good enough.

Reason seven: In certain subject areas, e.g., fine arts and the humanities, it is more difficult to identify measurable pupil behaviors.

Sure it's tough. Yet, because it is difficult in certain subject fields to identify measurable pupil behaviors, those subject specialists should not be allowed to escape this responsibility. Teachers in the fields of art and music often claim that it is next to impossible to identify acceptable works of art in precise terms—but they do it all the time. In instance after instance the art teacher does make a judgment regarding the acceptability of pupil-produced artwork. What the art teacher is reluctant to do is put his evaluative criteria on the line. He has such criteria. He must have to make his judgments. But he is loath to describe them in terms that anyone can see.

Any English teacher, for example, will tell you how difficult it is to make a valid judgment of a pupil's essay response. Yet criteria lurk whenever this teacher does make a judgment, and these criteria must be made explicit. No one who really understands education has ever argued that instruction is a simple task. It is even more difficult in such areas as the arts and humanities. As a noted art educator observed several years ago, art educators must quickly get to the business of specifying "tentative, but clearly defined criteria" by which they can judge their learners' artistic efforts (Munro, 1960).

Reason eight: While loose general statements of objectives may appear worthwhile to an outsider, if most educational goals were stated precisely, they would be revealed as generally innocuous.

This eighth reason contains a great deal of potential threat for school people. The unfortunate truth is that much of what is going on in the schools today is indefensible. Merely to reveal the nature of some behavior changes we are bringing about in our schools would be embarrassing. As long as general objectives are the rule, our goals may appear worthwhile to external observers. But once we start to describe precisely what kinds of changes we are bringing about in the learner, there is the danger that the public will reject our intentions as unworthy. Yet, if what we are doing is trivial, educators would know it and those who support the educational institution should also know it. To the extent that we are achieving innocuous behavior changes in learners, we are guilty. We must abandon the ploy of "obfuscation by generality" and make clear exactly what we are doing. Then we are obliged to defend our choices.

Reason nine: Measurability implies accountability; teachers might be judged on their ability to produce results in learners rather than on the many bases now used as indices of competence.

This is a particularly threatening reason and serves to produce much teacher resistance to precisely stated objectives. It doesn't take too much insight on the part of the teacher to realize that if objectives are specified in terms of measurable learner behavior, there exists the possibility that the instructor will have to become *accountable* for securing such behavior changes. Teachers might actually be judged on their ability to bring about desirable changes in learners. They should be.

But a teacher should not be judged on the particular instructional *means* he uses to bring about desirable *ends*. At present many teachers are judged adversely simply because the instructional procedures they use do not coincide with those once used by an evaluator when "he was a teacher." In other words, if I'm a supervisor who has had considerable success with open-ended discussion, I may tend to view with disfavor any teachers who cleave to more directive methods. Yet, if the teacher using the more direct methods can secure learner behavior changes which are desirable, I have no right to judge that teacher as inadequate. The possibility of assessing instructional competence in terms of the teacher's ability to bring about specified behavior changes in learners brings with it far more assets than liabilities to the teacher. He will no longer be judged on the idiosyncratic whims of a visiting supervisor.

Rather, he can amass evidence that, in terms of his pupils'
actual attainments, he is able to teach efficiently.

Even though this is a striking departure from the current
state of affairs, and a departure that may be threatening to the
less competent, the educator must promote this kind of accountability rather than the maze of folklore and mysticism
which exists at the moment regarding teacher evaluation.

*Reason ten: It is far more difficult to generate such precise
objectives than to talk about objectives in our customarily
vague terms.*

Here is a very significant objection to the development of
precise goals. Teachers are, for the most part, far too busy to
spend the necessary hours in stating their objectives and measurement procedures with the kind of precision implied by this
discussion. It is said that we are soon nearing a time when we
will have more teachers than jobs. This is the time to reduce the
teacher's load to the point where he can become a professional
decision-maker rather than a custodian. We must reduce public
school teaching loads to those of college professors. This is the
time when we must give the teacher immense help in specifying
his objectives. Perhaps we should *give* him objectives from
which to choose, rather than force him to generate his own.
Many of the federal dollars currently being used to support
education would be better spent on agencies which would produce alternative behavioral objectives for all fields at all grade
levels. At any rate, the difficulty of the task should not preclude its accomplishment. We can recognize how hard the job
is and still allocate the necessary resources to do it.

*Reason eleven: In evaluating the worth of instructional schemes
it is often the unanticipated results which are really important,
but prespecified goals may make the evaluator inattentive to the
unforeseen.*

Some fear that if we cleave to behaviorally stated objectives which must be specified prior to designing an instructional
program, we will overlook certain outcomes of the program
which were not anticipated yet which may be extremely important. They point out that some of the relatively recent "new
curricula" in the sciences have had the unanticipated effect of
sharply reducing pupil enrollments in those fields. In view of
the possibility of such outcomes, both unexpectedly good and

bad, it is suggested that we really ought not spell out objectives in advance, but should evaluate the adequacy of the instructional program after it has been implemented.

Such reasoning, while compelling at first glance, weakens under close scrutiny. In the first place, really dramatic unanticipated outcomes cannot be overlooked by curriculum evaluators. They certainly should not be. We should judge an instructional sequence not only by whether it attains its prespecified objectives, but also by any unforeseen consequences it produces. But what can you tell the would-be curriculum evaluator regarding this problem? "Keep your eyes open," doesn't seem to pack the desired punch. Yet, it's about all you can say. For if there is reason to believe that a particular outcome may result from an instructional sequence, it should be built into the set of objectives for the sequence. To illustrate, if the curriculum designers fear that certain negative attitudes will be acquired by the learner as he interacts with an instructional sequence, then behavioral objectives can be devised which reveal whether the instructional sequence has effectively counteracted this affective outcome. It is probably always a good idea, for example, to identify behavioral indices of the pupil's "subject-approaching tendencies." We don't want to teach youngsters how to perform mathematical exercises, for example, but to learn to hate math in the process.

Yet, it is indefensible to let an awareness of the importance of unanticipated outcomes in evaluating instructional programs lead one to the rejection of rigorous pre-planning of instructional objectives. Such objectives should be the primary, but not exclusive, focus in evaluating instruction.

While these eleven reasons are not exhaustive, they represent most of the arguments used to resist the implementation of precise instructional objectives. In spite of the very favorable overall reaction to explicit objectives during the past five to ten years, a small collection of dissident educators has arisen to oppose the quest for goal specificity. The trouble with criticisms of precise objectives isn't that they are completely without foundation. As conceded earlier, there are probably elements of truth in all of them. Yet, when we are attempting to promote the wide-scale adoption of precision in the classroom, there is the danger that many instructors will use the comments and objections of these few critics as an excuse from thinking clearly about their goals. Any risks we run by moving to behavioral goals are miniscule in contrast with our current state of confusion regarding instructional intentions. The objections against behaviorally stated goals are not strong enough. To secure a dramatic increase in instructional effectiveness we must abandon our customary practices of goal-stating and turn to a framework of precision.

References

Arnstine, D. G. (1964), The language and values of programmed instruction: part 2. *The Educational Forum, 28.*

Jackson, P. W. (1966), *The way teaching is.* Washington, D. C.: National Education Association.

Komisar, P. B., and McClellan, J. E. (1965), Professor Arnstine and programmed instruction. Reprint from *The Educational Forum.*

Mager, R. F. (1962), *Preparing instructional objectives.* San Francisco: Fearon Publishers.

Munro, T. (1960), The interrelation of the arts in secondary education. In *The creative arts in American education.* Cambridge, Mass.: Harvard University Press.

Functional Basis for Using
Objective-based Programs

Even though the value of instructional objectives is now more widely accepted, conflicts still exist over the use of objective-based programs. Generally, the concerns are the result of misunderstanding as to what objective-based programs are and are not. Niedermeyer and Sullivan (1977) present eight major concerns about objective-based programs and respond to them similarly to the way that Popham (1973) responded to arguments against instructional objectives.

1. *We already have our own objectives.* Research indicates that the use of traditional nonobjective-based instructional material is not successful in producing student achievement (Baker, 1968; Popham, 1971). Although teachers develop objectives and materials, data are rarely collected measuring the performance levels on the objectives. Providing teachers with instructional objectives or matching test items is likely to

improve pupil attainment. For successful mastery of objectives, instructional materials and procedures need to be designed for each objective. Teachers need appropriate materials to go along with the classroom objectives. Objective-based programs provide materials that are specially designed for each objective.

2. *We are going to develop our own instructional materials.* Instructional materials that produce successful student performance require great amounts of time, money, and experience. Highly trained and specialized research teams typically spend several years developing a program that covers several grades for one subject. Most school systems are unable to finance a successful instructional development program. By using objective-based programs, school systems are able to afford the experience and specialization of a trained staff necessary for an effective instructional program.

3. *Objective-based instruction differs little from traditional instruction.* Research indicates that teachers sometimes expose students to content and information without having objectives clearly in mind (see Niedermeyer and Sullivan, 1977). With objective-based instruction students may be given individualized practice, feedback, and self-correction based on specific objectives. Guidelines are built into objective-based programs to enable teachers to focus on specific objectives rather than extraneous ones. Objective-based programs help teachers define objectives and develop student proficiency.

4. *Objective-based programs stifle teachers' creativity.* The intention of the use of objective-based program resources is to produce successful student performance of the objectives. Objective-based programs do not require teachers to use all the materials that are provided. When used, the program provides teachers with a method of assessing student achievement during the course to see which objectives are mastered. Teachers have the option to reject a program, but generally, teachers are pleased to use the materials since they have been pretested and revised for classroom use.

5. *We don't use single programs because we match programs to individual learning styles.* Recently, special attention has been given to individualized instruction programs. Objective-based instruction allows teachers to identify students who have not mastered particular objectives easily. If current materials are not effective, then alternate instructional procedures are

used accordingly (Bloom, 1976). Objective-based programs allow students to learn at their own pace with direct practice and continuous feedback.

6. *Much of the testing in objective-based programs is unnecessary.* Many teachers object to the use of regular tests to place students and instead rely on their own judgment. However, research suggests that teachers often place students at inappropriate levels of achievement (Hanson and Schutz, 1975). Diagnostic testing in an objective-based program provides a systematic basis for measuring student performance. The testing provides information about those students who have mastered the objectives and about the ones who need additional instruction. Teachers using objective-based programs get the benefit of hearing and/or observing many responses that would be lost in a traditional learning environment and are often able to assess student proficiency more accurately.

7. *Objective-based programs mean accountability.* Many school systems are now required to produce successful student achievement levels and to explain what is being learned in quantitative terms. Previous methods for testing accountability have often been inaccurate. A well developed objective-based program provides a basis for making instructional accomplishments visible and for demonstrating them to appropriate evaluation committees. Since the classroom programs are verified and objectives assessed, it is likely that student performance will be satisfactory to help schools meet appropriate standards.

8. *Instructional accountability is exclusively the responsibility of teachers.* Since each school system is evaluated individually, instructional accountability should be shared by all levels of education. Many school systems provide teachers with instructional programs and materials and leave the responsibility for student success with the teachers. Objective-based supervision helps to spread responsibility and indicate areas for improvement. The shared responsibility among teachers and administrators helps school systems maintain high standards of instruction.

Below are three additional issues concerning the use of instructional objectives and objective-based programs that Dr. Popham and Niedermeyer and Sullivan (1977) do not discuss. They are taken from Kibler, Barker, and Miles, 1970 and Kibler, Barker, and Cegala, 1970a.

1. *Prespecifying the objectives for a unit of instruction that a teacher has not previously taught.* This is indeed a complex task. But it has been our experience that a procedure such as the following can reduce some of the complexity and result in a fairly complete set of objectives for succeeding times the course is taught.

A. Specify a set of objectives in general terms. These objectives should be based on an analysis of post-instructional performance expectancies and pre-instructional performance capabilities.

B. Specify more precise objectives for each unit as it occurs.

C. Evaluate the results of each unit, and base the objectives for the following units on these results.

D. Identify and record objectives that are achieved in addition to those prespecified for each unit.

This procedure is essentially a crude technique for testing hypotheses regarding objectives, identifying unpredicted objectives, and determining criteria for appropriate levels of performance. Thus, experience with the first attempt at a course is used to develop a set of precise objectives for succeeding presentations.

2. *Deciding whether all students should be required to achieve the same objectives.* With the increasing emphasis on individualized instruction, this decision is indeed relevant. Our viewpoint is that for most courses in public school, industrial, and undergraduate education, all students should achieve a common set of goals. This does not, however, preclude the possibility of specification of instructional objectives for *individual* student achievement. Opportunities should be available for students in many of these courses to go beyond the basic requirements to pursue individual areas of interest. One technique that has been employed frequently involves each student's stating specific objectives. Such a procedure seems quite appropriate when one of the teacher's objectives is for students to be able to identify and acquire behavioral competencies of personal concern.

3. *Deciding whether all students should be required to achieve the same level of mastery for each objective.* This issue is related to the previous one. Educators are evaluating the value of using the *norm-referenced* evaluation and grading system, in which students are assessed on the basis of their

performance relative to the group, and the *criterion-referenced* system, in which students are evaluated according to their achievement of specified criteria—regardless of how the group performs. The norm-referenced system is presently the more widely used system, although the criterion-referenced system is growing in popularity. (Further discussion of these systems is presented in Chapter 7.)

Without clearly defined objectives and performance criteria for measuring attainment of the objectives, the norm-referenced system is probably the more reasonable method available for assessing student achievement. However, given specific objectives and evaluation criteria, the practice of measuring the relative achievement of the objective may be open to question. Much has been written on this issue recently, and very likely the increased use of instructional objectives is to a great extent responsible for the dialogue.

Some educators feel that the purpose of education is not to determine who learns more or less of a given subject matter, but rather to see to it that all students learn what is considered necessary. From this viewpoint, the criterion-referenced system would be the desirable choice. This approach does not negate the possibility of providing the opportunity for students to go beyond the basic required objectives. The latter possibility may be extremely important to a more widespread acceptance of criterion-referenced evaluation, since relative achievement information (presently provided by norm-referenced evaluation and grading) is employed for a large variety of seemingly vital functions. School grades are used as a basis for selecting students for college, major areas of study, graduate school, honors programs, scholarships, and postschool employment; for retaining students in school; for influencing students' occupational choices; and for recording progress toward certificates and degrees. They are also used as incentives and rewards. Accordingly, some kind of information regarding a student's academic performance relative to other students is necessary. Possibly standardized academic ability or achievement tests eventually can provide such information and the results of instructional evaluation could be used only for determining the effectiveness of instruction when students have achieved specified objectives.

Two generalizations regarding this issue seem appropriate.

When mastery of an objective is vital to the achievement of subsequent objectives (for example, some language and computational skills are essential to much of what follows in school and after school), then all students should be required to master the objective fully. When subsequent performance demands are not so clear-cut, it may be appropriate to permit students to achieve varying levels of mastery of an objective—but with some minimum criterion.

The other generalization involves the domain of evaluation in education. The three primary functions of evaluation in instruction are to provide information regarding 1) student achievement of instructional objectives; 2) the success of instruction in getting students to achieve objectives; and 3) student achievement and ability that can be used for academic and occupational selection. Although both the norm-referenced and criterion-referenced systems can provide information for the three functions, the criterion-referenced system probably is a more desirable procedure for accomplishing the first and second functions, and the norm-referenced system is more appropriate for meeting the third function. The different amounts of time students spend in reaching criteria could provide information for function 3 within a criterion-referenced system, but such a practice may result in an overemphasis on speed of acquisition and an underemphasis on retention and transfer.

It is our position that a criterion-referenced system should be employed for the basic fundamentals of instruction, and that all students should be required to meet the standards considered necessary for postinstruction performance. In addition, opportunities for students to go beyond the required standards should be provided, and the results of students' performance in these areas, plus the results of standardized achievement and ability tests, should be used to satisfy the functions for which grades are presently used.

The Relationship of Instructional Objectives
to Participants in the Educational Process

Instructional objectives benefit all individuals involved in the teaching-learning process, particularly students, teachers, administrators, school boards, and parents (Kibler and Barker, 1970). The purpose of this section is to illustrate how the use of instructional objectives applies to those persons directly or indirectly involved with the educational process.

Instructional Objectives and Students

Research concerned with the transfer of learning indicates that students generally do not apply learned skills or knowledge to practical situations unless the teacher specifically demonstrates the application. The popular phrase in academic circles that reflects this body of research is "teach for transfer." The teacher attempting to implement this strategy makes desired behaviors explicit and specifies the variety of conditions under which the behaviors or skills may be applied after they have been adequately learned. When instructional objectives are given directly to students, the exact behaviors desired and the conditions under which the behaviors are to be exhibited are specified. By being given instructional objectives, students do not have to guess what is expected of them in the learning setting. Learners may spend their time acquiring behaviors specified by the teacher rather than attempting to infer what the teacher expects of them. It stands to reason that if students know what is expected of them, they will expend less random energy studying unimportant material and will concentrate on learning important skills.

One final value of giving instructional objectives to students is intangible yet very important. It is the sense of security a student experiences when knowing what specifically is expected in a course and the conditions under which one will be expected to exhibit competencies. Psychologists suggest that generalized fears cause greater emotional anxiety than specific, well-defined fears. Instructional objectives can help students understand specific requirements of a course and also reduce the amount of generalized anxiety about course requirements.

Reducing anxiety for students is especially important with new federal mandates. Ten years ago educational programs were primarily concerned with the public school system, but today equal educational opportunities are included for all segments of society. Recently, Public Law 94-142 required equal educational programs and facilities for all handicapped children. These children, with mainstreaming, need special objectives to reduce their fears and to enable them to adapt more easily. Specialized objectives are also beneficial for programs with the elderly, the very young, and for programs with a wide range of age and subject areas.

Instructional Objectives and Teachers[1]

The value of instructional objectives to the teacher is dependent, of course, upon the level of instruction, the subject matter of the course, the nature of the school system, and countless other variables related to the instructional environment. However, there appear to be at least two values of objectives (for teachers) that remain constant in most teaching situations. First, objectives prompt teachers to determine the most significant aspect of the subject matter to be learned. At the college level, students often joke that a specific course (e.g., Advanced Theories of Learning) is, in reality, a course in Professor X. In other words, the professor makes no attempt to define critical elements of subject matter related to the course but only talks about theories of learning of personal interest. In rare situations a course in Professor X may be desirable and useful, but from a curriculum viewpoint such a course creates a void of information in a student's educational background that might be important in the future. If teachers discipline themselves to analyze the content of specific courses for which they are responsible, the problem of majoring on minors or dwelling on unimportant issues will become less critical. It should be emphasized at this point that this value of objectives is not held universally by all educators.

A second value of objectives to teachers is their aid in establishing criteria for the measurement of classroom achievement. Most teachers have had the experience of teaching a unit in a course and then spending long, torturous hours attempting

---

[1] Teachers interested in an opportunity to share their instructional objectives with other teachers and to obtain copies of objectives used by other teachers will want to read Appendix D, which briefly explains a program to encourage the exchange of instructional objectives.

to devise ways of measuring what the students have learned. Teachers often find that had they approached the subject matter in a slightly different manner or modified instructional strategies, the measure of classroom achievement could have been greatly simplified and improved (i.e., made more reliable and valid). Instructional objectives require teachers to specify criteria for acceptable behaviors and to determine in advance how acceptable performance will be measured. Thus measurement in the classroom may be improved.

A side effect of these two values for teachers is similar to that experienced by students. The teacher who is confident 1) that the subject matter being presented is of prime importance and 2) that measurement of achievement is efficient and appropriate to course goals is more secure in his/her position and, consequently, is usually more satisfied with personal professional contribution.

Instructional Objectives and Administrators

Instructional objectives are important at two levels of administration. The administrator responsible for designing and coordinating curricula (in conjunction with the instructional staff) relies on instructional objectives to ensure that content and subject matter are covered adequately and that there are minimal overlaps between courses, especially within related areas. The use of instructional objectives also promotes consistency and a thread of continuity among related courses. Continuity is especially important in a series of courses where there is an introductory section followed by an intermediate or advanced section.

When the administrator is supervisor and teacher-evaluator, instructional objectives help in a different way. The objectives 1) suggest the degree of progress desired at a point in the course in light of the predetermined sequence of units and 2) help determine whether teachers are pursuing adequately the goals of the course. When the instructional objectives are developed by the teacher, they give the supervising administrator insight into the teacher's philosophy and course goals. This freedom to develop individual objectives is more prevalent at higher levels of instruction.

Instructional Objectives and School Boards

One of the persistent problems in education is to obtain adequate funds for the maintenance of a quality educational program. *School board* refers to the group of citizens who control funds in an educational setting. In the college context the term *board of trustees* or perhaps the *committee on education* would be substituted for the term *school board.*

In order to defend an existing budget or demonstrate the need for increased funds, administrators and teachers often are required to describe the existing educational program or some proposed addition to the curriculum. It is difficult to provide the board with a verbal or verbal-pictorial representation of the learning situation as it really exists because board members are often far removed from the classroom. However, when a school system requires instructional objectives for courses, it is possible to demonstrate the content of courses in objective form to a school board and thus demonstrate, more concretely than might otherwise be possible, precisely what learning achievements occur in a given classroom on a given day. This concrete representation of the educational program often may have some communicative or persuasive value to a school board. Thus, instructional objectives may help educate and persuade those persons in charge of educational funds.

Instructional Objectives and Parents

Parents are often neglected as participants in the educational process. However, parents are becoming increasingly concerned about the quality of education in the school and are, therefore, becoming more involved with their children's educational growth and classroom problems. When students are given instructional objectives, the parents may also elect to study them and determine what behaviors are expected of their child during the school year. Although we are unaware of the existence of such a practice, we feel that a procedure of periodically sending home a list of the actual objectives achieved by a student would be a marked improvement over the grade report-card procedure commonly used. Parents could thereby gauge the progress of their child at intervals during the year to help ensure that proper levels of achievement are being maintained. It is, of course, desirable that parents confer with teachers as well as with their children about educational achievement, but the presence of instructional objectives can serve to make parents more familiar with the child's desired growth and, in some instances, indicate areas where the child needs special help outside of the classroom.

Parents may be overly concerned about minor points in the curriculum that were stressed when they were in school. The specification of *major* objectives can help parents emphasize and reinforce the goals being sought by the teacher and can alleviate tendencies on the part of some parents to stress relatively unimportant concepts to their children.

Summary

In this chapter we have attempted to present several reasons for using instructional objectives. The rationale examined the use of instructional objectives from rational, empirical, and functional perspectives. The rational perspective offered logical reasons for using instructional objectives. The empirical perspective included a brief review of research concerned with the effects of instructional objectives on student learning. Overall, research findings suggest that students learn more effectively when presented with instructional objectives. Finally, the functional perspective was examined to help resolve some of the controversy over the use of instructional objectives and objective-based programs. In the last part of the chapter the relationship between instructional objectives and various participants in the educational process was examined.

REFERENCES

Baker, E. L. The differential effect of giving behavioral and nonbehavioral objectives to teachers on the achievements of their students. Paper presented at annual meeting of the California Educational Research Association, Berkeley, California, 1968.

Bassett, R. E. The effects of student training in the use of behavioral objectives, and knowledge of test performance on learner achievement in a modified mastery learning course in speech communication. Unpublished doctoral dissertation, Florida State University, 1973.

Block, J. H. Introduction to mastery learning: theory and practice. In J. H. Block (Ed.), *Mastery learning: theory and practice.* New York: Holt, Rinehart and Winston, Inc., 1971.

Block, J. H., and Anderson, L. W. *Mastery learning in classroom instruction.* New York: Macmillan, 1975.

Bloom, B. S. Learning for mastery. *Evaluation Comment* 1, 1968.

———. *Human characteristics and school learning.* New York: McGraw-Hill, 1976.

Boardman, D. E. The effect of students' advanced knowledge of behavioral objectives on their achievement in remedial chemistry. Unpublished doctoral dissertation, University of California at Los Angeles, 1970.

Brown, J. L. The effects of revealing instructional objectives on the learning of political concepts and attitudes in two role-playing games. Unpublished doctoral dissertation, University of California at Los Angeles, 1970.

Carroll, J. A model of school learning. *Teachers College Record* 64, 1963, 723-733.

Dawley, L. T., and Dawley, H. H. Incidental and intentional learning of economic information in beginning typewriting. *Perceptual and Motor Skills* 38, 1974, 337-338.

Duchastel, P. C., and Brown, B. R. Incidental and relevant learning with instructional objectives. *Journal of Educational Psychology* 66, 1975, 481-485.

Duchastel, P. C., and Merrill, P. F. The effects of behavioral objectives on learning: a review of empirical studies. *Review of Educational Research* 43, 1973, 53-69.

Ebel, R. L. Behavioral objectives: a close look. *Phi Delta Kappan* 52, 1970, 171-173.

Eisner, E. W. Educational objectives: help or hindrance? *School Review* 75, 1967, 250-260.

Elam, S. The age of accountability dawns in Texarkana. *Phi Delta Kappan* 51, 1970, 509-515.

Gagné, R. M. Educational objectives and human performances. In J. D. Drumboltz (Ed.), *Learning and the educational process.* Chicago: Rand McNally, 1965a.

Hanson, R., and Schutz, R. *The effects of programmatic R&S on schooling and the effects of schooling on students.* Technical Report 53, SWRL Educational Research and Development, Los Alamitos, California, 1975.

Hauck, W. E., and Thomas, J. W. The relationship of humor to intelligence, creativity and intentional and incidental learning. *Journal of Experimental Education* 40, 1972, 52-54.

Hausdorf, H. Empirical determination of the relative importance of educational objectives. *Journal of Experimental Education* 34, 1965, 97-99.

Houston, W. R., and Warner, A. R. The competency-based movement: origins and future. *Educational Technology* 17, 1977, 14-19.

Jenkins, J. R., and Deno, S. L. Influence of knowledge and type of objectives on subject-matter learning. *Journal of Educational Psychology* 62, 1971, 67-70.

Kibler, R. J., and Barker, L. L. Stating objectives in speech communication. *National Association of Secondary School Principals* 54, 1970, 30-39.

Kibler, R. J., Barker, L. L., and Cegala, D. J. Behavioral objectives and speech communication instruction. *Central States Speech Journal* 21, 1970a, 71-80.

———. A rationale for using behavioral objectives in speech instruction. *The Speech Teacher* 19, 1970b, 145-256.

Kibler, R. J., Barker, L. L., and Miles, D. T. *Behavioral objectives and instruction.* Boston: Allyn and Bacon, Inc., 1970.

Kibler, R. J., Bassett, R. E., and Byers, J. P. Behavioral objectives and communication instruction: state of the research. *Human Communication Research* 3, 1977, 278-288.

Lessinger, I. M. Accountability in public education. *Today's Education* 59, 1970, 52-53.

Macdonald, J. B., and Walfron, B. J. A case against behavioral objectives. *The Elementary School Journal* 71, 1970, 119-128.

Morse, J. A., and Tellman, M. H. Effects on achievement of possession of behavioral objectives and training concerning their use. Paper presented at AERA Convention, Chicago, April 1972.

Niedermeyer, F. C., and Sullivan, H. J. Prospects for school acceptance of objectives-based instructional programs. *Educational Technology* 17, 1977, 20-25.

Ohrtman, W. S. (principal investigator). *Special education resources location analysis and retrieval system* (SER-LARS). King of Prussia, Pa.: National Learning Resource Center of Pennsylvania, Federal Grant 300-75-0034, 1976.

Popham, W. J. Performance tests of teaching proficiency: rationale, development and validation. *American Educational Research Journal* 8, 1971, 105-117.

———. *Criterion-referenced instruction.* Belmont, Calif: Fearon Publishers, 1973.

Rothkopf, E. Z., and Kaplan, R. Exploration of the effect of density and specificity of instructional objectives on learning from text. *Journal of Educational Psychology* 63, 1972, 295-302.

Tiemann, P. W. Student use of behaviorally-stated objectives to augment conventional and programmed revisions of televised college economics lectures. Paper presented at the meeting of the American Educational Research Association, Chicago, 1968.

Tobias, S., and Duchastel, P. C. Behavioral objectives, sequence, and anxiety in CAI. Tech Memo No. 57. Tallahassee: CAI Center, Florida State University, 1972.

Wolk, S. The influence of meaningfulness upon intentional and incidental learning of verbal material. *Cognition* 2, 1973, 189-193.

2

The General Model
of Instruction

After completing this chapter, the learner should be able to:

1. State the major premise and specific assumptions underlying the general model of instruction;
2. Draw the general model of instruction and briefly describe each component in the model;
3. Describe the relationship between the educational level of learners and the difficulty of specifying/measuring instructional objectives.

In the previous chapter, we examined several key issues in the controversy over the use of instructional objectives. It is our belief that much of the confusion and controversy over their use stems from a lack of information that integrates instructional objectives systematically with other key components of the instructional process. Accordingly, we have organized our examination of instructional objectives in a manner designed to illustrate 1) how objectives relate to key components of the instructional process, 2) the implications for teachers and students when instruction incorporates objectives, and 3) how objectives may be used to improve instruction throughout various stages of the entire instructional process. To provide coherence in meeting these goals, we have devoted subsequent chapters of this book to a discussion of instructional objectives as they relate to various components of a general model of instruction.

The *general model of instruction* is a procedural guide for the design, implementation, evaluation, and improvement of instruction. The model is applicable to all levels of education (e.g., elementary, secondary, higher), all subject matters (e.g., English, science, art, vocational), and any length of instructional unit (e.g., one hour, one week, one semester).

The major premise underlying the model is that the goal of teaching is to maximize the efficiency/effectiveness and minimize the anxiety with which students achieve specified objectives. More specific assumptions of the model are that *most effective* instruction occurs when:

1. Maximum communication exists between teacher and learner regarding the objectives and goals of instruction.
2. Learners are provided with instructional objectives tailored to individual needs and capabilities.
3. Learners are provided with instructional experiences that are designed to help them achieve goals stated in instructional objectives.
4. Learners are given the opportunity to progress and, if need be, to recycle through instructional units at their own pace until mastery of instructional objectives is achieved.

Even if it is not possible for instruction to reflect all of these assumptions, the general model of instruction can be used effectively to guide instructional designers and teachers through the major steps in designing and carrying out instruction. The model provides an overall structure with which to view and study the instructional process.

The general model of instruction does not propose to tell teachers what they should teach or what specific instructional methods they should employ. It simply presents a guide for the teacher to use in deciding 1) what he/she would like students to learn, 2) what instructional methods to employ, and 3) how to determine whether students have learned what was intended. The range of possible objectives from which a teacher can select is nearly limitless. There are dozens of different methods of teaching, and each teacher generally employs each method somewhat differently. A wide variety of equally valid means of evaluation also exists. Each individual teacher must make decisions regarding objectives, instructional procedures, and evaluation on the basis of several factors, such as 1) personal views of what is important for students to learn, 2) the community and institution in which teaching occurs, 3) the type of students involved, and 4) personal preferences and capabilities regarding instructional methods and resources. The general model of instruction is primarily concerned with helping teachers teach what, and how, they want to teach as well as possible.

Although the model itself has not been validated experimentally for instructional efficiency, several of the prescriptive principles contained in it are derived from empirical research. The model is based on a technology of instruction that has been developed over the past several years from research and development work in three areas—experimental psychology, military training, and programmed instruction. The four individuals who have contributed most to the specific model presented in this document are Robert Gagné (1965a, 1965b, and 1977), Robert Glaser (1965), W. James Popham (1973), and Ralph W. Tyler (1950).

A flow diagram of the model is shown below. Each step in the model actually composes a body of knowledge with which anyone concerned with instruction should be intimately familiar. On the following pages each component of the model is explained briefly, and several of the major factors to consider at each step are presented. The material is designed to provide an overview of the instructional process. In subsequent chapters each component of the model is discussed more completely, particularly as it relates to the use of instructional objectives.

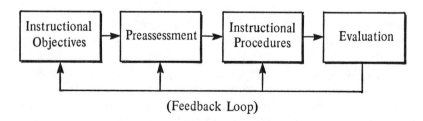

(Feedback Loop)

FIGURE 2-1.   A General Model of Instruction

Instructional Objectives

Preparing instructional objectives is probably the most important step in the entire model, for the instructor must decide what to teach. The four major factors involved in preparing objectives—selection, classification, analysis, and specification—are discussed briefly below.

Selection

The selection of appropriate objectives usually is based on the following factors: 1) what the students are able to do before beginning the unit; 2) what the students should be able to do in subsequent instructional units and what they should be able to do after completing their education; and 3) the available instructional resources, including the instructor's capabilities with the subject matter.

Classification

The taxonomies by Bloom and others (1956) and Krathwohl and others (1964) are useful in making sure that the objectives selected are of the level or type actually desired. For example, by classifying objectives in the cognitive domain into taxonomic categories, the instructor can determine whether the desired behaviors are knowledge, comprehension, application, analysis, synthesis, or evaluation. Gagné (1977) and Guilford (1967) also have produced useful systems for classifying human performance.

Analysis

Once an objective has been selected, the instructor should analyze the behaviors that students will be expected to demonstrate to indicate achievement of the objective. The actual components to be examined in a behavioral analysis are 1) the important stimuli to which a student responds; 2) the important responses made; and 3) the criteria that the responses must meet to be considered successful.

Analysis can be performed by observing students who have already achieved the objective as they exhibit the desired behavior. For example, these students can be interviewed and the products (tests, papers, etc.) they have produced can be examined. No matter how the behavioral analysis is conducted, a list should be compiled of the instructional objectives that clearly and completely prescribe the behaviors students are to acquire as a result of completing the instruction.

Specification

Instructional objectives are most valuable when they contain the following three elements recommended by Robert Mager in *Preparing Instructional Objectives* (1975):

1. A description of the type of *observable behavior* that the student will be asked to employ in demonstrating mastery of the objective (e.g., "to write," "to solve," "to identify," "to describe orally"). Terms such as "to know," "to understand," and "to appreciate" must be avoided, since they do not refer to observable behavior.
2. A description of the important *conditions* under which the student will be expected to demonstrate achievement of the objective (e.g., time limits, materials or equipment that will be available, or special instructions).
3. The *criterion* that will be used to evaluate the success of the student's performance (e.g., must get 70 percent correct, correctly apply three principles, complete the task in fifteen minutes, or correctly identify eight out of ten).

At this point, we need to emphasize that the function of these instructional objectives is for *planning* instruction, not for *informing* others of instructional intentions. Planning objectives are more detailed than the objectives used typically for the purpose of communicating goals to others. Several types of extremely important objectives are difficult to measure and, thus, are difficult to specify in behavioral terms. As a matter of fact, it seems that the more significant an objective is, the more difficult it is to measure. Examples of objectives that fall into the difficult-to-specify-and-measure category are those in the areas of problem solving, creativity, attitudes, and values. The only apparent solution is for such objectives to be specified as clearly as possible and for the instructor to be as resourceful as he/she can be in developing evaluative measures, including attitude inventories and creativity tests.

Such objectives (e.g., "to shape favorable attitudes toward your subject matter and toward learning") should *not* be eliminated because they are difficult to measure; they should be included, and the instructor should work toward improving means of measurement. Samples of some of these types of objectives are included in Appendix A.

Preassessment

Prior to beginning a unit of instruction, it is desirable to assess students to determine 1) how much they already know; 2) whether they have the necessary behavioral capabilities for the instruction; and 3) the instructional activities that should be prescribed for each student. Of course, the assessment should be based on the specific instructional objectives designated for the unit. The results of this assessment should indicate 1) whether any students may *omit* any of the objectives in the unit; 2) whether any students should be required to master *prerequisite* skills before beginning the unit; and 3) what specific *instructional activities* should be provided for particular students. This course of action implies that individualized instruction or tracking procedures are available for the instructional event. However, it is frequently possible to require prerequisite behavioral competencies and omit objectives for individual students in group-paced instruction.

Instructional Procedures

After students are preassessed and adjustments are made, such as adding or eliminating objectives or requiring prerequisite learning, the instructional procedures are implemented. The design of the instructional procedures involves 1) selecting available instructional materials (e.g., books, films, or lesson plans); 2) preparing new instructional materials when necessary;

and 3) developing a sequential plan that appears to be the most efficient for achieving the stated objectives. Decisions should be based upon available research evidence whenever possible.

Evaluation

When students complete an instructional unit, they are evaluated to determine whether the instruction was successful in achieving the unit's objectives. Typically, evaluation involves using tests and other instruments to measure the acquisition of knowledge, skills, and attitudes. Frequently, it is necessary to specify or describe student achievement. This is usually a difficult task.

If the objectives have been specified clearly, test preparation is made easier. (We are not suggesting, however, that test construction itself is easy.) An important consideration in designing evaluative measures is that the instrument measure the exact behavior specified in the objectives. It also is important to note that the success of the instruction, as well as that of the students, is being evaluated.

In most instances in formal education, it is both desirable and feasible for almost all (if not *all*) students to master almost all (if not *all*) objectives. If individual students do not perform acceptably on all objectives, an explanation must be sought from among the following three reasons:

1. The unsuccessful students were inadequately prepared for the unit, which could mean that the objectives were unrealistic or that the students should not have begun the unit without prior training.
2. The unsuccessful students were not properly motivated to master the material.
3. The instruction was not designed properly, or insufficient time was provided for the students to master the objectives.

Changes in the objectives, the preinstruction procedures, the instruction, or the postinstruction evaluation should be made on the basis of the evaluational results (note the *feedback loop* on the flow chart). In addition to making changes based on observed results, instructors should make modifications on the basis of new developments in materials and techniques, new research findings, and changing values.

Feedback Loop

The feedback loop in the model serves two purposes. As already indicated, it serves to remind teachers that the results of evaluation may indicate that other components of the instructional process (e.g., objectives, preassessment procedures, instructional procedures) need modification. Another purpose of the feedback loop is concerned with the issue of providing students with feedback about their progress in learning. Ammons' (1956) exhaustive review of the literature on the effects of knowledge of performance suggests that students learn more rapidly and reach higher levels of performance when provided with knowledge of performance. Recent research reported by Bloom, Hastings, and Madaus (1971) on formative and summative evaluation procedures also supports Ammons' generalization. Moreover, Airasian (1971) and Duchastel and Merrill (1973) have suggested that instructional objectives may facilitate learning by providing feedback concerning student progress. For example, Airasian (1971) has suggested that upon completion of a formative test,[1] a student should be provided with immediate feedback of the objectives corresponding to the test items answered correctly. By identifying unmastered objectives, the student may then devote energies to corrective activities that may lead to overcoming deficiencies in performance. Of course, such a strategy assumes that the student is provided with instructional objectives, multiple test attempts, and encouragement to work toward predetermined mastery levels. We will discuss the concepts of multiple testing procedures and mastery learning more fully in Chapter 7.

Application of Instructional Objectives to Specified Educational Levels

Now that we have examined the general model of instruction, it is important to explain how instructional objectives are used with differing educational levels. Personal experience and developmental research suggest that individuals acquire capacities

---

[1] A formative test is given during the course for feedback purposes. It is *not* a test of terminal performance.

to perform different skills and intellectual operations at various periods of development (McDonald, 1965; McCandless and Trotter, 1977; DeCecco, 1974). Behavior patterns for a given individual vary in rate of development and may vary substantially from individual to individual (Edwards and Scannell, 1968). Moreover, students of learning also may recall that there are a variety of types of learning, that these different types of learning may be sequential, and that a given type of learning may be contingent upon previously learned behaviors (Glaser, 1962; Gagné, 1965a and 1965b).

Obviously, the extent and kind of information to be acquired, applied, analyzed, synthesized, and evaluated differ between preschool and graduate programs. The specific psychomotor skills and attitudes to be acquired also vary as a function of educational level.

Instructional objectives must be viewed in light of many different variables in the educational setting. Perhaps one of the more critical variables that affects their use is the level of education for which objectives are intended. Several important distinctions among objectives at differing educational levels should be pointed out.

Figure 2-2 emphasizes a *general tendency*: as the educational level increases, the complexity of behaviors (and objectives) required increases. But the relationship suggested in Figure 2-2 is just a tendency. We do not intend to imply a one-to-one relationship regarding educational level and task complexity. Anyone who has taught in an elementary classroom knows that small children are capable of performing some very complex tasks. However, the child in the first grade most likely will be given objectives that emphasize the acquisition of basic skills frequently implemented through drill and practice, while students in higher education situations frequently will be given objectives that emphasize applying, organizing, problem solving, and other concept manipulation tasks. The point is, it frequently becomes more difficult to formulate objectives and measure the outcomes of instruction as the educational level increases.

The relationship between grade level and observable behaviors is exceedingly complex and cannot be expressed completely in a simple graph. It is possible to express a *general tendency* for the two to be related, as shown in Figure 2-3.

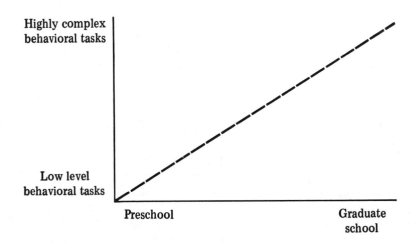

FIGURE 2-2. Generalized Relationship Speculated Between
Grade Levels and Complexity of Tasks Required

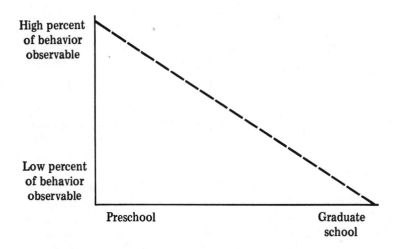

FIGURE 2-3. Generalized Relationship Speculated Between
Percent of Behavior Observable and Grade Levels

Again, a *tendency* is being expressed in Figure 2-3; there is no intention to imply a one-to-one relationship. Figure 2-3 emphasizes that the behaviors desired at lower educational levels frequently are observable (e.g., psychomotor behaviors), while behaviors desired at higher levels tend to be less observable (often affective and cognitive behaviors).[2] An objective for a child of kindergarten age, such as "place the square block in the square hole," involves considerably less complex skills than an objective for a postdoctoral seminar, such as "given the desired characteristics of a proposed synthetic plastic, develop a material that meets the desired specifications and provide a projected cost analysis for full-scale production."

It follows from the above contentions that the learner increases (or should increase) responsibility for learning quite rapidly as educational levels increase. Increasing the complexity and decreasing the observable behaviors as a function of educational level suggest the learner has little option but to become a more independent learner.

The higher the level of instruction, the more ambiguous and difficult to measure are the objectives. Many objectives at higher levels involve learning outside the context of the classroom. The result is that the observable behaviors are reduced for product evaluation. At lower levels most learning of desired skills occurs in class under the observation of the teacher. The measurement of these skills is made easier and more complete. Ideally, as the level of education increases, the relationship between instructional objectives and competencies required for real-life tasks also increases.

Realizing that such differences occur when using objectives at different instructional levels, teachers and administrators should attempt to adapt the specificity level and measurement level of objectives to appropriate grade levels or, better still, to the levels of individual students. Moreover, instructional objectives that are based on real-life competencies should be specified as soon and as frequently as possible. Measurement of objectives should be attempted at all levels, regardless of the complexity of the objective or the ambiguity of the task desired. Successful measurement is dependent not only on level of

---

[2] This observation was first suggested to one of the authors by William R. McKenzie of Southern Illinois University in a doctoral seminar in 1966.

instruction but on the creativity of the instructional planner and objective developer.

Summary

This chapter has focused on the general model of instruction. Each component of the model was described briefly and related to the use of instructional objectives. The second part of the chapter explained the use of instructional objectives at specific educational levels. Here is synthesis of the key components and concepts of the model:

> Premise of the Model: The goal of teaching is to maximize the efficiency/effectiveness and minimize the anxiety with which students achieve specified objectives.
>
> Functions of the model: 1) to guide instruction design and implementation; 2) to provide structure for viewing and studying instruction.

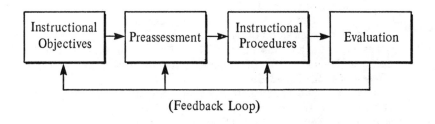

(Feedback Loop)

1. Select	1. Omit objectives	1. Select available materials	1. Evaluate instruction
2. Classify	2. Require prerequisites	2. Prepare new materials	2. Consider possible cause of failure: a) prerequisite b) motivation c) instruction d) objectives e) measurement
3. Analyze	3. Prescribe instruction	3. Develop a sequential plan	3. Modify to achieve 100% (or near) mastery

4. Specify
   1) Use feedback information to make needed modifications in other components of the model.
   2) Provide learners with knowledge of performance throughout instruction.

REFERENCES

Airasian, P. W. The role of evaluation in mastery learning. In J. Block (Ed.), *Mastery learning: theory and practice.* New York: Holt, Rinehart and Winston, 1971.

Ammons, R. Effects of knowledge of performance: a survey and a tentative theoretical formulation. *Journal of General Psychology* 54, 1956, 279-299.

Bloom, B. S., Hastings, J. T., and Madaus, G. F. *Handbook on formative and summative evaluation of student learning.* New York: McGraw-Hill, 1971.

Bloom, B. S. (Ed.), Engelhart, N. D., Furst, E. J., Hill, W. H., and Krathwohl, D. R. *Taxonomy of educational objectives—the classification of educational goals, Handbook I: cognitive domain.* New York: David McKay Company, Inc., 1956.

DeCecco, J. P. *The psychology of learning and instruction: educational psychology.* Englewood Cliffs, N. J.: Prentice-Hall, 1974.

Duchastel, P. C., and Merrill, P. F. The effects of behavioral objectives on learning: a review of empirical studies. *Review of Educational Research* 43, 1973, 53-69.

Edwards, A. J., and Scannell, D. P. *Educational psychology: the teaching-learning process.* Scranton, Pa.: International Textbook, 1968.

Gagné, R. M. Educational objectives and human performances. In J. D. Drumboltz (Ed.), *Learning and the educational process.* Chicago: Rand McNally, 1965a.

——. The analysis of instructional objectives for the design of instruction. In R. Glaser (Ed.), *Teaching machines and programed learning, II.* Washington, D. C.: National Education Association, 1965b.

——. *The conditions of learning,* 3rd ed. New York: Holt, Rinehart and Winston, 1977.

Glaser, R. (Ed.). *Training research and education.* Pittsburgh: University of Pittsburgh Press, 1962.

——. *Teaching machines and programmed learning, II.* Washington, D. C.: National Education Association, 1965.

Guilford, J. P. *The nature of human intelligence.* New York: McGraw-Hill, 1967.

Krathwohl, D. R., Bloom, B. S., and Masia, B. B. *Taxonomy of educational objectives—the classification of educational goals, Handbook II: affective domain.* New York: David McKay Company, Inc., 1964.

Mager, R. F. *Preparing instructional objectives,* 2nd ed. Belmont, Calif. Fearon Publishers, 1975.

McCandless, B. R., and Trotter, R. J. *Children: behavior and development,* 3rd ed. New York: Holt, Rinehart and Winston, 1977.

McDonald, F. J. *Educational psychology,* 2nd ed. Belmont, Calif.: Wadsworth, 1965.

Popham, W. J. *Criterion-referenced instruction.* Belmont, Calif: Fearon Publishers, 1973.

Tyler, R. W. *Basic principles of curriculum and instruction.* Chicago: The University of Chicago Press, 1950.

3

Instructional Objectives

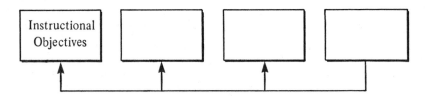

After completing this chapter, the learner should be able to:

1. Define a general objective and provide an example of a general educational objective;
2. Compare general objectives and instructional objectives in terms of specificity and purpose;
3. Define the terms *behavior* and *performance* as they apply to instructional objectives;
4. Identify and define five components of instructional objectives;
5. List and define ten action verbs that may be used in writing instructional objectives;
6. Describe three ways to determine what relevant conditions should be specified in an instructional objective;
7. Define *performance standard* and provide examples of different classes of performance standards;

8. Distinguish between performance standards that pertain to minimal level of mastery and that pertain to accuracy of performance.

In this chapter we will focus our attention on the first component of the general model of instruction—instructional objectives. First, the nature and function of instructional objectives are examined by distinguishing instructional objectives from other types of educational objectives. Second, three options are offered to you for learning how to write instructional objectives: 1) a textual reading option, where each component of instructional objectives is described and illustrated, 2) a programed text option, where components of instructional objectives are described and illustrated, and opportunity for practice and immediate feedback is provided, and 3) a combination option, where both the first and second options are taken. The chapter concludes with a discussion of selected difficulties encountered in specifying instructional objectives and with suggestions for reducing and/or eliminating these difficulties.

Different Types of Educational Objectives

Educational objectives are written at various levels of specificity and for different purposes. Figure 3-1 shows how objectives differ with respect to specificity and purpose.

General, nonspecific objectives.   Highly specific objectives.

Purpose: *Purpose:*
To indicate broad   To communicate instructional
goals of education.   intentions to learners.

General Educational Objectives

Instructional Objectives

FIGURE 3-1. Specificity/Purpose Continuum of Objectives

At the extreme end of nonspecificity are the very general objectives of educational institutions and broad educational programs. Most readers have been exposed to these types of objectives, which are called *general educational objectives.* A discussion of general educational objectives is included in *The Cardinal Principles of Secondary Education* (1937) and, more recently, in *The Central Purposes of American Education* published by the Educational Policies Commission of the National Education Association (1961). Examples of general educational objectives are "to make better citizens," "to advance humanity," and "to promote our cultural ideals." General objectives are important in the educational process because they relate the broad goals of education to the needs and expectations of society. General objectives often provide the philosophical guidance necessary for determining what specific instructional objectives ought to be included in a given curriculum. Even so, not all (but certainly some) general objectives have a one-to-one correspondence with instructional objectives for a given curriculum, since general objectives typically refer to the broad future goals that educators hope to achieve. This is not to say that instructional objectives have no relationship to future goals; rather, it is to say that often several instructional objectives in a given curriculum relate to one broad future goal that educators hope to achieve. Moreover, a reasonably large portion of general objectives typically refers to affective goals that often are not easily amenable to specification of learner development in observable, measurable terms.

At the other end of the educational objective continuum are specific instructional objectives—that type of instructional objective on which the general model of instruction presented in Chapter 2 focuses. Instructional objectives require specification of student learning in terms of observable, measurable behavior. An example of this type of instructional objective is:

> In a half-hour test at the end of the week, the student will be able to list the steps a bill follows through Congress, specifying the requirements for passage at each step. All steps must be included in the correct order, and the passage requirements must match the ones in the textbook.

Some educational objectives do not fit neatly into either the general or instructional objective category—such examples include outlines of objectives for elementary (Kearney, 1953) and secondary (French, 1957) educational levels, some objectives that have been developed for the language arts (Lazarus and Knudson, 1967), and the types of objectives included in the two volumes of the *Taxonomy of Educational Objectives* (Bloom et al., 1956, and Krathwohl et al., 1964). These objectives would be placed at varying points between general educational objectives and instructional objectives.

In particular, many (but not all) affective educational goals are appropriately placed between the general objective and instructional objective categories. Because of their dependence on the specification of observable, measurable behavior, instructional objectives most often are prepared for the cognitive and psychomotor domains. This is not to say that instructional objectives cannot be prepared for the affective domain, but many important affective objectives simply do not lend themselves to the type of specification illustrated by the instructional objective on page 48. Consequently, many affective (and some cognitive and psychomotor) objectives fall somewhere between general and instructional objectives and are used for a variety of purposes, including communicating instructional intentions to students and other teachers. Examples of these appear below:

1. The student seeks and reads books that are considered literary masterpieces.
2. The student watches educational television at home.
3. The student participates in extracurricular activities related to science class.
4. The student demonstrates a willingness to accept criticism from peers.
5. The student willingly complies to rules governing socially acceptable behavior in a variety of situations.
6. The student is able to discriminate various moods and meanings of classical music and explain his/her interpretations to others.

Writing Instructional Objectives

Most educational objectives, specific or otherwise, serve a valuable function in the educational process. The general model of instruction presented in Chapter 2 primarily focuses on the role and function of the more specific type of instructional objective, although less specific objectives also can be used within the model. However, to use the model most effectively, one must acquire the skills necessary to write instructional objectives for particular content areas.

——————*Branching Option Two*——————

At this point in the chapter we offer you three options for acquiring the skills necessary for writing effective instructional objectives. One option is for you to read carefully the section below entitled "Basic Concepts of Writing Instructional Objectives." This option is designed for those of you who prefer to read about the procedures for writing instructional objectives in a standard textbook format. To benefit maximally from this option, you should have the ability to read and assimilate concepts and subsequently to apply what you have read. In the text below, each component of an instructional objective is defined, discussed, and illustrated. A second option is for you to turn to page 59 and complete the program designed to teach you the components of instructional objectives and to provide you with examples of objectives, practice at writing objectives, and immediate feedback regarding the correctness of your responses. A third option is available; that is, of course, completing both of the first two options. We recommend the third option for maximum learning.

Basic Concepts of Writing Instructional Objectives

This section contains a behavioral analysis of what a student is expected to be able to do after successfully completing a unit of instruction. Other authors have used terms like *task description* or *task analysis* to describe similar information (Miller, 1962a, 1962b; Stolurow, 1963; Gagné, 1965a, 1965b, 1974, 1977; Taber, Glaser, and Schaefer, 1965; Lange, 1967; and Tyler, Gagné, and Scriven, 1967). Additional information on task analysis is included in Chapter 4. By *behavioral analysis*, we mean a study of the final behavior to be required of the student, broken down into its component parts. Before we examine each of the five parts of this final behavior, it may be valuable to review a few terms and concepts that will be used throughout this volume.

By *behavior*, we mean actions and movements that people can be observed (seen, heard, or felt) making. Thus, thinking, which involves electrochemical activity in the brain, is not considered behavior here, since the activity cannot be observed directly with the unaided senses. (However, such activity can be observed indirectly with mechanical devices such as an electroencephalograph.) Therefore, since instructional objectives must identify the action a person must perform, all instructional objectives require a psychomotor component.

Caution must be exercised, however, to avoid overemphasizing the "action" component of objectives; cognitive and affective objectives are concerned with characteristics of thinking and feeling that are themselves not directly observable. States of affection and acts of cognition are inferred from psychomotor acts. We do not see a person analyze a poem; we see or hear a report of the analysis. We do not see the mental activity of problem solving; we see tentative solutions to the problem. We do not see the emotional feelings a person experiences when listening to a favorite piece of music; we see the results of the emotional experience in verbal responses or facial expressions or in future selections of music to which one listens.

Actually, we are usually more interested in the characteristics of the products or actions that permit us to infer the type of mental activity that produced them than we are in the form of behavior that made them observable. However, since the only way we infer what happens "inside" people's heads or "hearts" is to look at what they do, we emphasize the observable actions. Objective evidence is required to determine whether a person has thought or felt in a particular way. If instructors were not concerned with making changes in students, they would not have to bother looking at behavior—but they do have that responsibility.

Performance is used in this book to refer to the result of a person's action that is evaluated to see whether he/she has successfully completed an objective. For example, if an objective is to build an electric motor that runs, the "performance" that is evaluated is whether the electric motor runs. Or, if an objective is to write a term paper according to a set of prescribed specifications, the term paper that the student turns in is what is evaluated and thus is considered performance. *Product* is frequently used as a synonym for *performance.*

You will see that these distinctions are necessary as we examine the components of instructional objectives. Gagné (1965a, 1965b, and 1977) has emphasized the importance of understanding the relationship between education and human performance. Human performance must be employed to determine what is *intended* to occur in education. It is also tied into an understanding of learning, since we infer that learning has taken place as a result of observing a change in performance. For example, suppose we observed two performance events separated by a few days. In the first event the student was presented with five sentences and was told to underline the verb in each of them; the student subsequently failed to perform the task satisfactorily. In the second event a similar set of instructions and list of sentences were presented to the same student. This time the student performed the task successfully. A *change* in the student's performance was observed, which might give us some basis for inferring that the student learned what verbs are and underlined them properly.

Now that some of these basic terms have been reviewed, we will analyze the component parts of the final performance that the student is expected to demonstrate as a result of completing an instructional unit. Instructional objectives should contain the following five elements:

1. *Who* is to perform the desired behavior (e.g., "the student" or "the learner").
2. The *actual behavior* to be employed in demonstrating mastery of the objective (e.g., "to write" or "to speak").
3. The *result* (i.e., the product or performance) of the behavior, which will be evaluated to determine whether the objective is mastered (e.g., "an essay" or "the speech").
4. The *relevant conditions* under which the behavior is to be performed (e.g., "in a one-hour quiz" or "in front of the class").
5. The *standard* that will be used to evaluate the success of the product or performance (e.g., "90 percent correct" or "four out of five correct").

Each of these components is identified in the objective shown below. The number of each *component* is *identified above* the appropriate portion of the instructional objective. Those words and phrases that are not a part of a specific component have no identification appearing above them.

4   1
| During the one-hour mid-term examination, | | the student | | will be
2   5   3
able | | to spell correctly | | 45 out of 50 | | words | | randomly selected
4
from the 200 words listed in Units one and two of the spelling book. | |
1   2   3   4
The student | | will write | | the words | as they are presented orally by the
5
teacher. | | In order to be correct, the spelling of each word must match

the spelling in the spelling book. |

Who Is to Perform the Desired Behavior. Determining the first component, the *who*, is easy. Obviously, you usually want the *student* to demonstrate the behavior. Other terms for those who may be asked to perform the desired behavior are *learner*, *pupil*, and *enrollee*.

The Actual Behavior to Be Employed. The second component of an instructional objective is the specific observable act or behavior that the learner is to perform. For example, the student may be instructed "to write," "to identify," or "to distinguish." Researchers working in task analysis have reported a necessity for "hard," "clear" *action verbs* to classify the behavior to be performed (Miller, 1962a and 1962b; Chenzoff and Folley, Jr., 1965; Gagné, 1977). Some of the action verbs used as operational guides are defined in the following list.

Definitions of Action Words[1]

1. *Identifying.* The individual selects (by pointing to, touching, or picking up) the correct object of a class name. FOR EXAMPLE: Upon

---

[1] Henry H. Walbesser, *Constructing Behavioral Objectives* (mimeographed). College Park, Md.: Bureau of Educational Research, University of Maryland, 1966. Reproduced by permission.

being asked, "Which animal is the frog?" when presented with a set of small animals, the child is expected to respond by picking up or clearly pointing to or touching the frog; if the child is asked to "pick up the red triangle" when presented with a set of paper cutouts representing different shapes, he is expected to pick up the red triangle. This class of performances also includes identifying object properties (such as rough, smooth, straight, curved) and, in addition, kinds of changes such as increase or decrease in size.

2. *Distinguishing.* Identifying objects or events which are potentially confusable (square, rectangle), or when two contrasting identifications (such as right, left) are involved.

3. *Constructing.* Generating a construction or drawing which identifies a designated object or set of conditions. EXAMPLE: Beginning with a line segment, the request is made, "Complete this figure so that it represents a triangle."

4. *Naming.* Supplying the correct name (orally or in written form) for a class of objects or events. EXAMPLE: "What is this three-dimensional object called?" RESPONSE: "A cone."

5. *Ordering.* Arranging two or more objects or events in proper order in accordance with a stated category. FOR EXAMPLE: "Arrange these moving objects in order of their speeds."

6. *Describing.* Generating and naming all of the necessary categories of objects, object properties, or event properties that are relevant to the description of a designated situation. EXAMPLE: "Describe this object," and the observer does not limit the categories which may be generated by mentioning them, as in the question, "Describe the color and shape of this object." The child's description is considered sufficiently complete when there is a probability that any other individual is able to use the description to identify the object or event.

7. *Stating a Rule.* Makes a verbal statement (not necessarily in technical terms) which conveys a rule or a principle, including the names of the proper classes of objects or events in their correct order. EXAMPLE: "What is the test for determining whether this surface is flat?" The acceptable response requires the mention of the application of a straightedge, in various directions, to determine touching all along the edge for each position.

8. *Applying a Rule.* Using a learned principle or rule to derive an answer to a question. The answer may be correct identification, the supplying of a name, or some other kind of response. The question is stated in such a way that the individual must employ a rational process to arrive at the answer. Such a process may be simple, as "Property A is true, property B is true, therefore property C must be true."

9. *Demonstrating.* Performing the operations necessary to the application of a rule or principle. EXAMPLE: "Show how you would tell whether this surface is flat." The answer requires that the individual

use a straightedge to determine touching of the edge to the surface at all points and in various directions.

10. *Interpreting.* The child should be able to identify objects and/or events in terms of their consequences. There will be a set of rules or principles always connected with this behavior.

The Result of the Behavior. The third component is the product, the performance, or the "what" the student is to do. Here are some examples of statements that include the first three components. The portion of the statement that appears in italics is the *result* of the behavior.

> The student writes *a sentence.*
> The learner walks *from point A to point B.*
> The student spells aloud *the word "simple."*

To determine the result you can expect from students in an educational setting, you must first decide what you *want* them to do as a result of instruction and then write instructional objectives identifying *what* behavior is to be performed.

There are several ways to determine what to include in instructional objectives. Some educators have found it useful to examine old tests, since they are one indication of what students can do after instruction. Others have interviewed students who have mastered the desired behavior, determining *what* their terminal behavior for a course was and *how* they performed it. Still others have observed a student actually demonstrating mastery performance or have observed a product produced (and the steps executed in producing it).

The Relevant Conditions Under Which the Behavior Is to Be Performed. What are the stimulus conditions to which the student will be expected to respond when demonstrating the desired behavior? To state this concern in less complex terms, "What are the *givens*, the *limitations*, the *restrictions* imposed on the student when demonstrating the terminal behavior?" Here are examples of some stimulus conditions that one might include in an instructional objective:

> "When presented with a typed list . . . "
> "Given a slide rule . . . "

"Upon reading Chapter 4 in *x* (insert name of textbook) . . . "
"With the use of class notes . . . "
"Without the use of class notes or other references . . . "

Now, let us turn to the question of how to determine the conditions under which the student will be expected to demonstrate mastery—conditions that are to be specified in the instructional objectives. Three suggestions are listed below:

1. Specify the information, tools, equipment, source materials, and anything else that will be available to the student to help in performing the terminal behavior required in the objective.
2. Specify the information, tools, equipment, source materials, and anything else that the student cannot use when demonstrating the terminal behavior.
3. List as many of the actual conditions as possible under which the student might be expected to demonstrate the terminal behavior in a real-life setting, and try to include as many of them in the objective as possible.

The Standard that Will Be Used to Evaluate the Success of the Product or Performance. We noted earlier in this volume that instructional objectives provide information regarding *how effectively* a student must perform in order to demonstrate adequate mastery of a prescribed behavior. Readers also may recall that specifying the expected level of performance was one of the steps identified for formulating instructional objectives. In this section we discuss the relevant characteristics of standards required for determining the adequacy of responses.

Standard or *criterion* as used here refers to a basis for evaluating the prescribed behavior. Suppose you were told that you must throw a baseball fifty feet to perform the task successfully. The standard specified for determining whether you performed the task of throwing the baseball adequately is *fifty feet.*

A *performance standard*, then, is a specified level of achievement used to identify individuals who have mastered a task acceptably. *Achievement* here refers to performance in terms of its adequacy. We determine achievement by answering this question: "How effectively was a given task performed in respect to a specified criterion or standard?"

Several of the reasons for including performance standards

in instructional objectives were mentioned previously. Performance standards help both teachers and students know where any given student is in any given program. They provide a minimal criterion and offer the potential of success to all students. Teachers find performance standards invaluable when determining the efficacy of their instructional programs. Mager (1975) indicates that when the minimum acceptable performance for each objective is specified, we have a performance standard to use in assessing instructional programs.

Classes of performance standards will now be considered. Various types of criteria may be used to determine mastery of given objectives. We will discuss some general types of performance standards as they relate to mastery level.

A specified level of mastery for objectives is generally determined arbitrarily, and it may have a wide range. In one case, the teacher may want the student to be able to list "all five steps similarly to the way they are stated in the textbook." In another case, the teacher may determine that, "given a 100-word typed message and five minutes in which to do the task, a student will type the message on a separate piece of paper; a successful, finished product will include no more than two errors (typing or any other kind of error)." In the latter case, the teacher has required almost perfect performance (although some typing teachers known to the authors would not agree that this criterion approximates perfect performance).

Minimal mastery level refers to what a student has to do to "win the game"—to achieve an objective successfully. The typing objective described above asked for minimal mastery. For another example, consider the following phrase:

... to be able to identify *at least five* characteristics of ...

Identification of five characteristics is the minimal mastery level acceptable in this example.

It is not possible to specify all the criteria for mastery level here because space is not available for a detailed discussion. However, here are some examples of different types of performance standards:

Minimum Number
 "... must list *four* steps. ... "
 "... write all *ten words* presented accurately. ... "

"... distinguish *three* main ideas...."

Percent or Proportion

" ... write (spell) accurately *100 percent* of the 10 words presented...."

" ... *list 80 percent* of the verbs appearing in a 200-word message...."

Limitation of Departure from Fixed Standard

"... must be correct to the *nearest percent*...."

"... must be within *five decibels* of...."

Distinguishing Features of Successful Performance

"... the radio plays within a *one-day period*...."

"... all balls on the paper are *colored red*...."

Examples of constraints are used above to specify performance standards in instructional objectives. They include limitations, restrictions, or confinements specifying or implying the conditions under which performance must occur to be successful. Consider the following example:

... to be able to walk a mile *within a ten-minute period.*

The constraint or restriction is *within a ten-minute period.* This phrase restricts the conditions (time limit) for successful terminal performance. One demonstrates mastery when one walks a mile "within a specified time period." Some examples of mastery level described above could be classified as constraints (e.g., " ... three out of four words.... "; " ... 80 percent.... "; " ... must be correct to the nearest percent.... ").

A potential point of confusion regarding constraints is related to the fact that they deal with conditions under which the behavior is to be demonstrated. In one sense, then, it is reasonable to classify such constraints under stimulus conditions that influence how the behavior will be executed satisfactorily. However, while constraints do specify limiting conditions regarding how the task is to be executed, the emphasis in using constraints as performance standards *is on how satisfactorily.* Note that the time-limit example above told the learner those conditions within which to operate to master the objective.

Accuracy of performance is another matter related to standards and one that borders on a semantic problem. Consider this example:

> Given 100 words presented orally by the teacher, the student will write down (spell) at least 80 percent of these words accurately. Accuracy will be determined by matching a student's responses on the written list to the correctly spelled words in the textbook (pp. x and y).

This objective has two standards worth distinguishing. The first standard, *"80 percent of these words,"* specifies the minimal level of mastery. The second states how the accuracy will be determined (i.e., how accurate responses can be defined operationally)—*"Accuracy will be . . . the textbook (pp. x and y)."* Many writers of objectives specify the performance standard (how effective), but not *how* the accuracy of performance will be determined. We encourage you to include both of these types of standards in your instructional objectives.

Suggestions to the teacher are offered here, for specifying performance standards.

1. Select carefully the actual criteria (and levels) for ascertaining mastery. Should you select criteria based on behavior levels that discriminate between successful and unsuccessful performance? Should you specify criteria low enough for everyone to master them easily (which will make you look like a great instructor) or high enough so that only the most able can master the performance standard (which will probably make you look like a poor teacher)?
2. Use a variety of measures, and where possible, describe alternative means for evaluating objectives. For some objectives, various behaviors such as "to identify" or "to distinguish" could be required for the same or similar material to be mastered. Why not change the level of the performance standard according to the task?

A Program for Writing Instructional Objectives[2]

The following pages contain
the program text option (#2)
described on page 50.

---

[2] Adapted from Donald J. Cegala, Robert J. Kibler, Larry L. Barker, and David T. Miles, "Writing Behavioral Objectives: A Programmed Article," *The Speech Teacher* 21, 1972, 161–168. Reprinted by permission of the Speech Communication Association of America.

Program Objectives. The desired terminal behavior to be performed upon completion of this program follows: Given a content area in a subject area of your choosing, you will write at least two instructional objectives for the content area, using the five components of instructional objectives correctly. Two secondary objectives that also may be attained as you work through the program include the following:

1. Given five minutes, you will list and define, in writing, the five basic components of instructional objectives.
2. Given two instructional objectives, you will identify and label, in writing, the five basic components of instructional objectives for each objective given.

Instructions for Programed Materials. The instructional program that follows is designed to help you learn to write instructional objectives in a systematic, step-by-step manner. The information about objectives is presented a bit at a time. Each bit or frame, unless otherwise specified, requires you to write down one or more answers. *Please use a blank sheet of paper as an answer sheet* because sufficient space is not provided in the program to write most answers. After you write your response to the frame, you will receive immediate feedback regarding the correctness of your answer. Accordingly, as you proceed through the program, the material on writing instructional objectives will be presented and, at the same time, you will receive feedback concerning appropriate answers about terms, principles, and concepts.

The frames begin at the top of each page and go down vertically to the bottom of the page. The first frame is followed by the second, third, and so on. Use a sheet of paper (different from your answer sheet) to cover (mask) the lower frames. Read each frame carefully, and then write your answer(s) on your sheet (another blank sheet of paper). After you have written your answer, slide the "masking paper" down the page, and you will receive feedback concerning your answer. Always go directly to the next successive frame, *unless you are instructed otherwise in the program.*

While going through this program, please try to remember that you are not taking a test but are learning about writing objectives. If, at times, it seems as though the material is

repetitious, this is because the program is constructed to reinforce principles or concepts learned earlier. Now, if you have
your two sheets of blank paper, you are ready to begin.

— 1

Instructional objectives are composed of five basic components. The first of these components, and easiest to
remember, is *who is to perform the desired behavior.*

— 2

Obviously, the student is to demonstrate the behavior.
When writing instructional objectives, other terms such
as "learner," "pupil," and "enrollee" may be used instead of the term "student." The label used is not important. What is important is that you specify

_____ .

— 3

You should have written: *who is to perform the desired behavior.* This is the first component of the five
components in instructional objectives.

— 4

The second component of instructional objectives is
*the specific observable act (or behavior) that the learner
is to perform.* For example, if you desired the learner to
draw a right triangle, then you should indicate the
specific behavior the learner is to perform, i.e., "to
diagram" or "to draw." The key point to remember
is that the behavior specified must be an observable act,
i.e., "to write," "to speak," "to list," etc.

— 5

The second component of instructional objectives is

_____ .

It is important to remember that the behavior specified
must be _____ .

— 6

You should have written: *the specific observable act (or
behavior) that the learner is to perform* and *an observable act.*

To help you keep these points in mind, you should begin to use "action verbs"[3] to indicate clearly what class of behavior is to be performed by the learner. Some examples of "action verbs" are:

1. identify	6. describe
2. distinguish	7. evaluate
3. construct	8. apply
4. name	9. locate
5. order	10. interpret

Compare these two objectives:

1. The student will know the five steps of reflective thinking.
2. The student will list in writing the five steps of reflective thinking.

Which objective more clearly specifies the desired behavior? _____

7

The correct response is objective 2: "The student will list in writing the five steps of reflective thinking."

Although we may have a reasonable degree of common meaning for the term "know," the question still remains: what do we mean when we say the learner should know the five steps of reflective thinking? Do we want the learner to apply the five steps, recite them, criticize them? It really is not clear. However, the phrase "list in writing," as it is used in objective 2 in Frame 6, indicates exactly what the learner is to *do* when demonstrating that he "knows" or "understands" the five steps of reflective thinking.

Which of the following objectives meets the criteria we have discussed thus far?

1. The student will understand the main points in a story.

---

[3] Much confusion exists here since action verbs are not always behavioral verbs. See Robert E. Robinson and David T. Miles, "Behavioral Objectives: An Even Closer Look," *Educational Technology*, 1971, 39–44, for a discussion of this topic. Also, for a listing of action verbs, see H. H. Harmes, *Behavioral Analysis of Learning Objectives* (West Palm Beach, Fla.: Harmes and Associates, 1969).

2. The student will write a five-sentence paragraph.
3. Draw a rectangle.
4. The student will know Ohm's law.
5. The student will orally apply principles of effective dramatic reading.

⑧

You should have selected objectives 2 and 5. If you were correct, go to Frame 10; if not, go on to Frame 9 (below).

⑨

Recall that the two components of instructional objectives discussed thus far are:

1. Who is to perform the desired behavior;
2. The specific observable act (or behavior) that the learner is to perform.

The first component now should be easy to remember. The student (pupil, learner, etc.) is the one who is to perform the behavior. Objective 3 in Frame 7 is incorrect because the first component of instructional objectives is missing: *who* is to perform the behavior. Written correctly, the objective should read: "The student will draw a rectangle."

In order to keep the second component in mind, you should become familiar with the "action verbs" listed in Frame 6. These "action verbs" clearly indicate what class of behavior the learner (student, pupil, etc.) is to perform. Therefore, objectives 1 and 4 in Frame 7 are incorrect because "know" and "understand" are not clear indicators of the *observable* behavior that the student is to perform. The terms "list," "define," or "apply" would have been much clearer because they indicate what observable behavior the student is to perform.

Go to Frame 12

⑩

Good show!! You were able to identify the correct objectives. You are almost ready to begin writing your own objectives. However, before moving to the third

component of instructional objectives, indicate below
the first two components of instructional objectives, and
list as many "action verbs" as you can.

1. _____

2. _____

1. _____   6. _____

2. _____   7. _____

3. _____   8. _____

4. _____   9. _____

5. _____   10. _____

─── 11

The correct responses are:

1. Who is to perform the desired behavior.
2. The specifc observable act (or behavior) that the
   learner is to perform.

1. identify   6. describe
2. distinguish   7. evaluate
3. construct   8. apply
4. name   9. locate
5. order   10. interpret

─── 12

The third component of instructional objectives is *the
product, performance, or result of the student's behavior.* The product, performance, or result of the student's behavior may be "a speech," "an essay," "a
successful dyadic interchange," etc. Some examples of
objectives containing this component and the other two
components discussed previously are listed below. The
third component is underlined in the objectives.

1. The student will identify in writing three causes of
   the Civil War.
2. The student will orally participate in a policy-making
   discussion using Dewey's five steps of reflective
   thinking.
3. The student will write a definition of democracy.

13

Before you attempt to write an instructional objective using the three components we have discussed thus far, let's be sure you remember what these components are.

By now you probably remember that the first two components are:

1. Who is to perform the behavior.
2. What is the specific observable act (or behavior) to be performed. What is the third component?
3. _____

You are correct if you said *the product (or performance or result) of the student's behavior.* If your response was incorrect, perhaps you should turn back to Frame 12 and reread the material before going on.

You are now ready to write an objective using the three components we have discussed thus far. Below is a list of six terms. Select three of the terms or phrases and order them to form an instructional objective.

1. know
2. the teacher will
3. define in writing
4. four steps in analyzing a proposition
5. the student will
6. understand

16

The correct response is 5, 3, 4.

The student will define in writing four steps in analyzing a proposition.

If you did not select 5, 3, 4, go to Frame 17; if you did select 5, 3, 4, go to Frame 18.

It seems you are having a few problems!

One set of alternatives you should have chosen between is "the teacher will" and "the student will." Although objectives sometimes are prepared for teachers, they most often are prepared for students. Therefore, the first component of your objective (who is to perform the behavior) should have been "the student."

You should have chosen one term among "know," "understand," and "define in writing." Recall that the terms "know" and "understand" really do not clearly indicate what the student is to *do* in demonstrating knowledge or understanding. The term "define in writing," however, specifically indicates what the student is to *do* in demonstrating competence. Therefore, "define in writing" is the correct response.

Recall the third component of instructional objectives is the product, performance, or result of the student's behavior. In this instance, the product to be produced is "the four steps in analyzing a proposition."

Go to Frame 18

18

By now you know that the second and third components of instructional objectives indicate what behavior the student is to perform and the end product or result of that performance. Although these components provide more clarity to students than most nonbehavioral objectives, it is often necessary to define further the behavior you are after by specifying *conditions you will impose upon the student when demonstrating the behavior.* In other words, what are the "conditions," the "limitations," the "restrictions" that are imposed on the student performing the stated behavior? Some examples of these conditions are:

1. Given one hour and a list of ten historical events . . .
2. Without use of the textbook or notes the student will . . .
3. After hearing a thirty-minute tape-recorded speech, the student will . . .
4. Without referring to an outline, the student will . . .

19

Below are three suggestions for determining the conditions under which the student will be expected to demonstrate the required behavior:

1. Specify the information, equipment, source materials, and anything else that will be available to the student when performing the required behavior.

2. Specify the information, equipment, source materials, and anything else that will not be available to the student when performing the required behavior.
3. List as many as possible of the actual conditions under which the student might be expected to demonstrate the terminal behavior in a real-life setting, and try to include as many of them in the objective as possible.

—————————————————————————————— 20

Given the preceding discussion, you should now be aware that the fourth component of instructional objectives is *the relevant conditions under which the behavior is to be performed.*

Let's see how successful we were in explaining this component. Which part of the objective below tells the student something about the conditions under which the behavior is to be performed?

1. Given a five-minute tape-recorded story and twenty minutes,
2. the student will write a paragraph retelling the events of the story.

If you selected:

> #1—go to Frame 22.
> #2—go to Frame 21.

—————————————————————————————— 21

Ooops! You selected the portion of the objective that reads: *the student will write a paragraph retelling the events of the story.*

You are probably still thinking of the second and third components of instructional objectives, the behavior to be performed and the product to be produced. Try not to get these components confused with *the relevant conditions under which the behavior is to be performed.* Perhaps you should turn back to Frame 18 and reread the material concerning the fourth component of instructional objectives.

When you have done that, go to Frame 23.

22

Congratulations! You selected the correct response—
*"Given a five-minute tape-recorded story and twenty
minutes . . . "* The portion of the objective you selected
indicated that the student would be given a story, the
relative length of the story, the mode of communication
it would be in, and the maximum time the learner would
have to perform the required behavior.

23

Does the objective below contain the fourth component
of instructional objectives?

Given a test, the student will demonstrate effective application of the rules of punctuation.

24

The answer is both yes and no.
    The objective does provide the student with some in-
formation about the condition under which to perform
the behavior, i.e., "given a test."
    However, some relevant conditions are not indicated
to the student. For example, will the test be oral or
written? Will the test be essay or multiple-choice? How
long will the test be? How much time will the student
have to complete the test?
    We might then rephrase the objective to read:

Given twenty written unpunctuated sentences and
one hour, the student will rewrite and correctly
punctuate at least sixteen sentences.

25

Look at the objective in Frame 24 again. Did you notice
anything different about this objective from other examples of objectives given thus far?
    Another component has been added to the objective.
Can you identify the component?

26

The fifth component added to the objective in Frame 24
is the *standard (or criterion) that will be used to evaluate
the success of the product or performance.*

The criterion in the example is: correctly punctuate at least sixteen sentences.

Look at the complete objective again:

> Given twenty written unpunctuated sentences and one hour, the student will rewrite and correctly punctuate at least sixteen sentences.

This component often is the most difficult to understand and use correctly. Let's examine the component more closely.

27

The *standard* or *criterion* refers to the basis for evaluating the prescribed behavior. Suppose you were asked to perform the following behavior:

> Run the fifty-yard dash.

As stated, you might infer that your performance would be evaluated on the basis of whether or not you were able to run fifty yards without stopping for a breather! But suppose we assumed that you were healthy and we desired to impose a time limit on your performance. The behavior might then be stated:

> Run the fifty-yard dash within eight seconds.

It is now clear that your running performance will be evaluated on the basis of the eight-second standard or criterion. This standard is the *minimum acceptable performance* for achieving the objective successfully.

28

Several types of criteria may be used to determine the minimum level of acceptable performance for objectives. Some examples of different types of performance standards appear below:

1. ... must list *four steps* ...
2. ... distinguish *at least three* main ideas ...
3. ... identify *80 percent* of the forms of support ...
4. ... must be correct to the *nearest percent* ...
5. ... must list *all* of the principles ...
6. ... must match in meaning *with the textbook* ...
7. ... must satisfy *80 percent* of the student's personal criteria ...
8. ... communicate an idea to *90 percent* of the students ...

———————————————————————————————— **29**

Does the objective stated below contain a standard?

Given a list of twenty incomplete sentences requiring adjectives, the student will write the adjectives to complete the sentences within fifteen minutes.

———————————————————————————————— **30**

If you answered "yes," you are probably confusing the fourth and fifth components of instructional objectives. Recall that the fourth component specifies the *relevant conditions* under which the behavior is to be demonstrated. True, such conditions do influence the manner in which the behavior will be executed satisfactorily, but they do not indicate *how satisfactorily* the behavior is to be performed.

Read the following objective:

Given a list of twenty incomplete sentences requiring adjectives, the student will write adjectives to complete the sentences within fifteen minutes.

The relevant conditions under which the behavior is to be performed are specified (i.e., given a list of twenty sentences requiring adjectives and a fifteen-minute time limit), but the standard or criterion to be used in *evaluating* performance is not included. For example, the objective does not state how many sentences must be written correctly or what standard will be used to judge correctness.

———————————————————————————————— **31**

Which objective below contains the standard or criterion component?

1. Given thirty minutes, the student will list in writing the types of government other than democracy and compare each type with democracy.
2. Given thirty minutes, the student will write an essay comparing and contrasting the democratic form of government with three other types of government. The product must contain at least one point of comparison and one point of contrast for each of the three types of government.

If you selected:

#1—go to Frame 33.
#2—go to Frame 32.

32

Good! You're getting the hang of it now. You recognized that the portion of the objective that stated: " . . . at least one point of comparison and one point of contrast for each of the three types of goverment" specified the standard or criterion for evaluation of student performance.

Go to Frame 34

33

Ooops! Look more carefully at the first objective. Note that the objective does not indicate how many types of government other than democracy the student must list. In other words, the minimum acceptable performance is not specified. Compare the first objective to the second one listed. The second objective indicates that *three types* of governments must be discussed. Note the last part of the second objective, " . . . the product must contain at least one point of comparison and one point of contrast for each of the three types of government." This part of the objective indicates the minimum standard of performance that the student must demonstrate.

Got it? Let's see . . .

Go to Frame 34

34

Which objective below contains the standard or criterion component?

1. Given one hour in class, the student will identify and describe in writing the role and function of freedom of speech in a democracy.
2. Given a list of ten famous scientists, the student will identify and describe in writing at least eight of the ten scientists' major contributions to knowledge.

If you selected:

#1—go to Frame 35.
#2—go to Frame 36.

35

You missed again! You selected: "Given one hour, the student will identify and describe in writing the role and function of freedom of speech in a democracy." Where is the standard in this objective?

Perhaps you should return to Frame 26 and reread the material concerning the fifth component of instructional objectives. Then go to Frame 37.

Then go to Frame 37.

36

Now you are getting it! " . . . at least eight of the ten scientists . . . " indicates an 80 percent criterion for performance.

Go to Frame 37

37

One more point is worth noting concerning the criterion component of instructional objectives. Consider the following objective:

> Given a thirty-minute essay quiz, the student will identify and describe in writing at least three of the similarities and differences between classical conditioning and instrumental conditioning. The essay will be evaluated on the extent to which it reflects points covered in assigned readings and class discussion concerning the two methods of conditioning.

The objective has two standards worth distinguishing. The first standard, "at least three," specifies the *minimum level* of acceptable performance. The second standard " . . . evaluated on the extent to which it reflects points covered in assigned readings and class discussion . . . ," states *how* accuracy will be determined. Many writers of instructional objectives specify the minimum level of acceptable performance, but not how the accuracy of the performance will be determined. You are encouraged to include both standards in writing instructional objectives.

Frame 38 provides some examples of objectives with both standards included.

38

1. Given thirty minutes, the student will draw a diagram indicating *at least five* major components of a plant cell and describe the relationships among the components *as presented in the textbook.*
2. Given one hour, the student will identify and describe in writing *at least five* methods for organizing messages *as they are presented in the textbook.*

3. Given thirty minutes, the student will describe in writing the scientific method and list *at least four* ways it differs from other methods of inquiry. *The product will be evaluated by the extent to which responses reflect information contained in assigned readings and class discussion.*

— **39**

Now you should be able to identify all five components of instructional objectives. Here is an instructional objective. Underline (or write on a separate piece of paper) each of the five components and label each component.

Given ten mixed numbers and proper fractions, the student will show in writing all the steps necessary to divide at least eight correctly.

— **40**

If this program has been successful, your response should look like this:

4

Given ten mixed numbers and proper fractions, | |

1   2   3

the student | | will show in writing | | all the steps

5

necessary to divide | | at least eight correctly.

1. Who is to perform the behavior.
2. The observable act (or behavior) to be performed.
3. The product, performance, or result of the behavior.
4. The relevant conditions under which the behavior is to be performed.
5. The standard (or criterion) used to evaluate the behavior.

— **41**

Since it is important for you to be able to identify all five components of instructional objectives before you begin writing your own objectives, try to identify the components in this objective:

Given five typewritten argumentative paragraphs and one hour, the student will identify in writing: 1) evidence, 2) warrant, 3) claim, 4) reservation, and 5) support for the warrant for each argument. Performance will be evaluated by the extent to which the student identifies correctly four of the five items listed above for each argumentative paragraph.

—————————————————————————————————— 42

The five components are:

4

Given five typewritten argumentative paragraphs

1   2

and one hour, | | the student | | will identify in

3

writing: | | 1) evidence, 2) warrant, 3) claim, 4)

reservations, and 5) support for the warrant for

each argument. | | Performance will be evaluated

5

by the extent to which the student identifies

correctly four of the five items listed above for

each argumentative paragraph.

1. Who is to perform the behavior.
2. The observable act (or behavior) to be performed.
3. The product, performance, or result of the behavior.
4. The relevant conditions under which the behavior is to be performed.
5. The standard (or criterion) used to evaluate the behavior.

—————————————————————————————————— 43

Now try to write an instructional objective. Suppose you were teaching students to conjugate irregular Spanish verbs. In addition, you are interested in students being able to translate the Spanish conjugates into English. Write an instructional objective expressing these ideas to your students.

———————————————————————————

———————————————————————————

———————————————————————————

———————————————————————————

———————————————————————————

———————————————————————————

44

The exact wording may vary, but you should have written something like this:

> Given a list of twenty Spanish irregular verbs and one hour, the student will conjugate at least eighteen verbs correctly (i.e., as shown in the textbook) and translate them to their correct English equivalents.

Well, how did you do?

Try writing an instructional objective for this situation:

Suppose you wanted students to apply some principles of effective adaptive listening that you had been discussing for a few days in class. To make life easier, let's say you had access to a ten-minute taped recording of an informative speech that had been recorded with interfering noise. In addition, you have a twenty-five-item multiple-choice test over material in the speech. "Put it all together," and write an objective for students including the relevant conditions stated above.

_____

_____

_____

_____

_____

45

Again, wording may vary, but essentially you should have written:

> Given a ten-minute tape-recorded informative speech and simultaneous presentation of interfering noise (e.g., white noise, music, conversation, etc.), the student will demonstrate application of principles of effective adaptive listening. Acceptable performance will be a score of 70 percent or better on a twenty-five–item, multiple-choice comprehension test over material contained in the speech.

46

If you have never written an instructional objective before, our guess is that you probably didn't do extremely well! Perhaps a little more practice is needed. Try writing an objective for this situation:

You have a unit on voice control in an oral interpretation class. The class will be taught how to apply specific criteria in evaluating proper voice control. You usually play a five-minute tape-recorded oral reading to your class and ask them to write a critique of the speaker's use of voice control to determine if the students can apply the evaluative criteria you have taught them. How would you specify this instructional intent in an instructional objective format?

47

Your objective should look something like this:

Given a five-minute tape-recorded oral reading and twenty minutes, the student will write a critique of the speaker's use of voice control in presenting the selection. The product will be evaluated by the extent to which the student employs the evaluative criteria presented in assigned readings and class lectures.

Getting better? Try writing an objective for the situation described in the next frame.

48

Try your hand at writing an objective for this situation:

You are teaching a course in acting and have a unit on improvisation. In the past you have required students to improvise assigned roles in specific situations. You would like to continue this practice because the students enjoy the assignment. Your main concern in the unit is that students are convincing (i.e., believable) in the roles that they improvise.

49

Your instructional objective should look something like this:

Given a written statement describing a situation involving two of the following person-roles—a parent, student, teacher, administrator, spouse—the student will improvise an assigned person-role for six minutes with a classmate. Performance will be evaluated by the extent to which the class agrees that the improvisation was believable as indicated by responses on a rating form.

How did you do on that one? If you are experiencing problems, don't worry. Writing good instructional objectives is not easy; it requires time, effort, and *practice*. Hopefully, you now have the skills that will allow you to practice writing instructional objectives. Go to it! Happy writing and teaching!!

THE BEGINNING . . .

Difficulties Encountered in Specifying Objectives

Problems will be encountered as you specify instructional objectives. We have identified a few of these difficulties so that you may watch for them as you formulate your objectives. Some of the problems identified here were first encountered in a thoughtful report prepared by Ammerman and Melching (1966).

Sometimes an instructor fails to specify important performance standards because the information is not readily available for an instructional decision. Be careful not to be satisfied with less important objectives just because measuring devices are available or because certain behaviors are easy to measure. If a complex learning operation is important but not included in an objective, break it down into its component parts and develop standards to assess the level of mastery of each part (see Chapter 4). If we do not have standards for successful performance, we should begin developing them, and now is as good a time as any.

Another potential difficulty is associated with utility. What is the mastery for? While it may be convenient to measure whether three out of four steps of x process are included in a written statement, maybe all four steps must be demonstrated actually to use the process; mastery of three steps may be of little or no value. Moreover, the value of mastery becomes even clearer when the total process of learning is considered. Today's instructional objectives are used to create tomorrow's preinstructional evaluation for the next higher level of instruction.

A problem somewhat related to utility is making the objectives relevant to the task (i.e., derived from the known work requirements for a given job or learning task). Those activities in which students are required to engage that are not required in a work situation or in a higher-order learning level may be of limited value. There is also the possibility of stating instructional objectives (and particularly performance standards) that are related primarily to a testing situation rather than to the next set or ultimate learning operation to be acquired.

Still another problem is related to the teacher's knowing what objectives are desired and communicating that knowledge to the student. If the instructor has not specified instructional objectives, one could infer that he/she has not decided what students be able to do as a result of instruction. Missing performance standards or other incomplete information in instructional objectives invites similar inferences from outside observers, such as colleagues, parents, and administrators.

A difficult but important task for the teacher is to arrange instructional objectives and performance standards for given instructional objectives into a priority list. It is critical to learning to arrange the priorities for given tasks into an efficient order. It is just as important to arrange the priority of performance standards (and to use several of them) to determine the mastery required for a given objective. Regarding students' mastery of objectives, it also is important for the teacher to remember that the potential measurement error in evaluation procedures should be considered. Errors in measurement may account for a student's meeting the criterion "accidentally" or failing to meet it when expected to.

Summary

This chapter has focused on the first component of the general model of instruction—instructional objectives. Instructional objectives were distinguished from other types of educational objectives in terms of specificity and purpose. Three options were then offered for learning how to write instructional objectives. The first option described and illustrated each component of instructional objectives in a textbook format. The second option consisted of a programed text that described and illustrated components of instructional objectives and, in addition, provided opportunity for practice in writing instructional objectives. The third option, which provided for maximum learning, consisted of both the first and second options. The chapter concluded with a discussion of selected difficulties encountered in specifying instructional objectives and offered suggestions for reducing those difficulties.

REFERENCES

Ammerman, H. L., and Melching, W. H. *The derivation, analysis, and classification of instructional objectives.* Alexandria, Va.: George Washington University, 1966.

Bloom, B. S. (Ed.), Engelhart, N. D., Furst, E. J., Hill, W. H., and Krathwohl, D. R. *Taxonomy of educational objectives—the classification of educational goals, Handbook I: cognitive domain.* New York: David McKay Company, Inc., 1956.

The cardinal principles of secondary education. Bulletin No. 35. Washington, D. C.: U.S. Government Printing Office, 1937.

Chenzoff, A. P., and Folley, J. D., Jr. *Guidelines for training situation and analysis.* Technical report NAVTRADEVCEN 1218-4, Contract Number N 61339-1218. Valencia, Pa.: Applied Science Associates, Inc., 1965.

Educational Policies Commission. *The central purpose of American education.* Washington, D. C.: National Education Association, 1961.

French, W., and Associates. *Behavioral goals of general education in high school.* New York: Russell Sage Foundation, 1957.

Gagné, R. M. Educational objectives and human performances. In J. D. Krumboltz (Ed.), *Teaching and the educational process.* Chicago: Rand McNally, 1965a.

_____. The analysis of instructional objectives for the design of instruction. In R. Glaser (Ed.), *Learning machines and programmed learning, II.* Washington, D. C.: National Education Association, 1965b.

_____. *Essentials of learning for instruction.* Hinsdale, Ill.: The Dryden Press, 1974.

_____. *The conditions of learning,* 3rd ed. New York: Holt, Rinehart and Winston, 1977.

Gagné, R. M., and Briggs, L. M. *Principles of instructional design.* New York: Holt, Rinehart and Winston, 1974.

Haynes, J. L. *Organizing a speech: a programmed guide.* Englewood Cliffs, N. J.: Prentice-Hall, Inc., 1973.

Kearney, N. C. *Elementary school objectives.* New York: Russell Sage Foundation, 1953.

Krathwohl, D. R., Bloom, B. S., and Masia, B. B. *Taxonomy of educational objectives—the classification of educational goals, Handbook II: affective domain.* New York: David McKay Company, Inc., 1964.

Lange, P. (Ed.). *Programmed instruction*, Part II. The Sixty-sixth Yearbook of the National Society for the Study of Education. Chicago: University of Chicago Press, 1967.

Lazarus, A., and Knudson, R. *Selected objectives for the English language arts: grades 7-12*. Boston: Houghton Mifflin, 1967.

Mager, R. F. *Preparing instructional objectives*, 2nd ed. Belmont, Calif.: Fearon Publishers, 1975.

Miller, R. B. Analysis and specification of behavior for training. In R. Glaser (Ed.), *Training research and education*. Pittsburgh: University of Pittsburgh Press, 1962a.

_____. Task description and analysis. In R. M. Gagné (Ed.), *Psychological principles in system development*. New York: Holt, Rinehart and Winston, 1962b.

Stolurow, L. M. *Teaching by machine*. Washington, D.C.: U.S. Government Printing Office, 1963.

Taber, J. I., Glaser, R., and Schaefer, H. H. *Learning and programmed instruction*. Reading, Mass.: Addison-Wesley, 1965.

Tyler, R. W., Gagné, R. M., and Scriven, M. *Perspectives of curriculum evaluation*. American Educational Research Association. Monograph Series on Curriculum Evaluation. Chicago: Rand McNally, 1967.

4

Classifying and Sequencing Instructional Objectives: Behavioral Taxonomies and Task Analysis

After completing this chapter, the learner should be able to:

1. State three reasons for using a classification scheme in preparing instructional objectives;
2. Describe and critique the role of behavioral taxonomies in sequencing objectives for instruction;
3. Describe the procedures for conducting task analysis;
4. State at least four reasons for using task analysis in designing instruction;
5. Prepare a taxonomic classification of objectives for a selected unit of instruction in one's own subject area;
6. Construct a task analysis on at least one objective in the taxonomic classification prepared in objective 5 above.

So far we have presented a general overview of instructional objectives and how they relate to other components of our model. In addition, we have discussed various types of objectives and procedures for writing them. In this chapter we will extend our treatment of objectives by examining how they may be used to plan and sequence instructional units.

As suggested in Chapter 3, a critical first step in preparing instructional objectives is to determine what kinds of learning outcomes are desired for a given unit of instruction. The term learning outcome refers to the observable behavior that is desired of the learner (see Gagné, 1974; Gagné, 1977; Gagné and Briggs, 1974). Clearly, the writer of instructional objectives must have in mind what learners are expected to demonstrate as an outcome of instruction before objectives can be written. This point may seem so obvious that it hardly requires attention. However, anyone who is even vaguely familiar with the instructional process knows that there are an infinite variety of learning outcomes that may be sought by educators, parents, and students. Given the vast amount and diversity of potentially desirable learning outcomes, it is necessary for educators to specify those outcomes that are most relevant to given units of instruction. By specifying these learning outcomes educators can more effectively communicate their intentions to each other, to parents, and to students.

The requirement to specify learning outcomes places an additional, but necesary, burden on teachers, curriculum planners, and other individuals involved in the design and/or implementation of instruction. Educators seek ways to maximize efficiency and effectiveness in specifying desired learning outcomes at all levels of instructional planning. One such approach has been to seek ways of classifying varied learning outcomes into more clearly defined clusters, or groupings, to make the task of specification more orderly and manageable. Probably the most familiar scheme used by educators for this purpose is the one representing the three domains of behavior with which education typically has dealt—cognitive, affective, and psychomotor. These behavioral domains still represent only broad classifications of human behavior and educational objectives. Within each of these behavioral areas it is possible to classify objectives into progressive levels of development.

Bloom and others (1956), Krathwohl and others (1964), and Simpson (1972) have conducted systematic surveys of educational objectives in the cognitive, affective, and psychomotor domains and have prepared taxonomies for these three classes of behavior. These taxonomies are included in this chapter. For the moment, it is important to emphasize that by using the three-category scheme or others like it (see Gagné and Briggs, 1974; Harrow, 1972; Merrill, 1971; Walbesser, 1965), educators are able to classify various kinds of learning outcomes into groupings of human behavior that share common dimensions.

This classification allows for greater ease and clarity in identifying a wide variety of specific and general learning outcomes that may be relevant to educational planning and development.

Classification schemes do not solve all of the problems facing educators who are trying to specify learning outcomes. Research results conflict when evaluating the classification of hierarchal structures (Seddon, 1978). Bloom's classification of test items has been criticized because of its category placement difficulties. However, no taxonomy is universally perfect and Bloom's seems more useful than other available taxonomies. No matter how useful a classification scheme may be, there is always the potential for ambiguity when attempting to make discrete classifications of complex human behavior. There are instances of phenomena that should or could be classified into more than one category. For example, consider an instructional objective such as "to be able to present an original five-minute speech in front of the class without exhibiting stage fright." This objective includes as many as three different types of learning outcomes related to various domains of human behavior. Psychomotor skills are involved in meaningful sound production, while certain attitudes about speaking before others are also implied (i.e., affective domain). In addition, comprehending and repeating information contained in the speech suggests the inclusion of relevant cognitive behaviors. Although classification schemes do not always allow educators to specify learning outcomes in discrete categories, the overall pragmatic values of such schemes generally outweigh the drawbacks. This chapter will discuss methods of classification schemes that may be used to prepare and sequence objectives for implementing instructional strategies.

An Aid to the Preparation of Instructional Objectives

In Chapter 3 we emphasized the preparation of specific types of instructional objectives. The reason for this emphasis is our belief that most of our readers are teachers who are concerned about preparing objectives that contain highly specific instructional intentions. Most instructional objective writers do not begin their work at this highly specific level, especially if they are preparing objectives for relatively large units of instruction (e.g., one week, one semester). Instead, most individuals begin instructional planning by stating general objectives that are desired for a given unit of instruction, and gradually become more specific as the unit takes shape.

Regardless of the initial level of desired specificity, a key question on which the instructional objective writer must focus is: *what type of learning outcome do I want?* If the traditional three-category scheme is used, then the type of learning outcome is classified primarily as cognitive, affective, or psychomotor. An alternative scheme would suggest that the learning outcome be labeled as an intellectual skill, information acquisition, cognitive strategy, motor skill, or attitude (see Gagné and Briggs, 1974; Gagné, 1977). The particular classification scheme used is probably less important than that some scheme be employed. Why? We have already suggested that a classification scheme (i.e., taxonomy) allows the instructional objective writer to categorize a wide range of learning outcomes into more manageable clusters that share some common dimensions. This is important for several reasons.

According to Gagné (1977), classification of objectives is necessary for planning and sequencing of instruction. He convincingly argues that different internal and external conditions of learning are associated with various types of learning outcomes and, therefore, it is necessary to specify those various learning outcomes in order to plan instruction effectively. (We will examine this aspect of classifying objectives later in this chapter.)

As indicated in previous chapters, instructional objectives require teachers to specify learner performance in terms of observable, measurable behaviors. It is, of course, easier to meet this requirement for some learner behaviors than it is for others. For example, it probably would not be difficult to specify and measure the observable behaviors necessary to adjust a carburetor correctly, but it would be difficult to specify and measure the observable behaviors associated with an appreciation for classical music. Part of the ease or difficulty in specifying observable, measurable behaviors is related to the nature of the behavior with which you are concerned; that is, the kind of learning outcome desired (e.g., cognitive, affective, psychomotor). We already have suggested that behaviors in the cognitive and psychomotor domains often are more easily specified in observable, measurable terms than behaviors in the affective domain.

Another issue pertains to the type of behavior required *within* a particular domain rather than *across* the three domains. The issue is concerned with the level of the behaviors (in terms of complexity or difficulty) as classified within each behavioral taxonomy. In general, it is less difficult to specify performance in observable, measurable terms for lower-level behaviors (e.g., knowledge, awareness, physical set) than it is for higher-level behaviors (e.g., synthesis, characterization, complex overt response). Since most units of instruction focus on several learner behaviors ranging from the very simple to the very complex, it is important for teachers to specify instructional objectives for learning outcomes at all levels of difficulty.

There is a tendency for instructional objective writers to overemphasize objectives for the lower-level behaviors because it generally is less difficult to specify objectives for these levels than for higher levels. The oversimplification prompts some critics to argue that the use of instructional objectives results in trivial learner outcomes. However, an overemphasis on lower-level behaviors is not a fault of instructional objectives; rather, it is a fault of the person writing the objectives. An objective writer may avoid this pitfall by using a behavioral taxonomy when writing instructional objectives. The taxonomy will serve as a guide in determining 1) what is the appropriate level of behavior associated with a desired learning outcome and 2) the extent to which objectives for a unit of instruction reflect various levels of behavior. In essence, behavioral taxonomies serve to guide the objective writer in specifying the appropriate type (i.e., level) and variety of behaviors desired for given units of instruction.

For your convenience we have included a taxonomy for each of the traditional types of learning outcomes identified in education. At this point a careful examination of the taxonomies may be helpful. Following the taxonomies, suggestions are given as to how they may be used to prepare and classify instructional objectives.

Cognitive Domain

When developing the taxonomies, Bloom's committee found that the majority of objectives in the educational literature were related to the cognitive domain. The objectives classified as cognitive emphasize intellectual, learning, and problem-solving tasks. Behaviors in this domain range from performing simple recall tasks to placing previously learned material into new contexts and synthesizing bodies of learned information. The following abstract of the taxonomy of educational objectives for the cognitive domain indicates the levels of cognitive behaviors under which objectives may be classified, provides brief definitions for each level, and, in most cases, provides sample objectives for the specific level of behavior. (Additional taxonomies for the cognitive domain include: Gagné and Briggs, 1974; Merrill, 1971; Walbesser, 1965.)

A Condensed Version of the Cognitive Domain of the Taxonomy of Educational Objectives[1]

Knowledge

1.00 KNOWLEDGE

Knowledge, as defined here, involves the recall of specifics and universals, the recall of methods and processes, or the recall of a pattern, structure, or setting. For measurement purposes, the recall situation involves little more than bringing to mind the appropriate material. Although some alteration of the material may be required, this is a relatively minor part of the task. The knowledge objectives emphasize most the psychological processes of remembering. The process of relating is also involved in that a knowledge test situation requires the organization and reorganization of a problem such that it will furnish the appropriate signals and cues for the information and knowledge the individual possesses. To use an analogy, if one thinks of the mind as a file, the problem in a knowledge test

---

[1] From David R. Krathwohl, Benjamin S. Bloom, and Bertram B. Masia, *Taxonomy of Educational Objectives—The Classification of Educational Goals, Handbook II: Affective Domain.* New York: David McKay Co., Inc., © 1964, pp. 186–193. Reprinted by permission of David McKay Co., Inc. (This is an abstract of Benjamin S. Bloom et al., *Taxonomy of Educational Objectives—The Classification of Educational Goals, Handbook I: Cognitive Domain.* New York: David McKay Co., Inc., 1956.)

situation is that of finding in the problem or task the appropriate signals, cues, and clues that will most effectively bring out whatever knowledge is filed or stored.

1.10   Knowledge of Specifics

The recall of specific and isolable bits of information. The emphasis is on symbols with concrete referents. This material, which is at a very low level of abstraction, may be thought of as the elements from which more complex and abstract forms of knowledge are built.

1.11   Knowledge of Terminology. Knowledge of the referents for specific symbols (verbal and nonverbal). This may include knowledge of the most generally accepted symbol referent, knowledge of the variety of symbols that may be used for a single referent, or knowledge of the referent most appropriate to a given use of a symbol.

> To define technical terms by giving their attributes, properties, or relations.
> Familiarity with a large number of words in their common range of meanings.[2]

1.12   Knowledge of Specific Facts. Knowledge of dates, events, persons, places, etc. This may include precise and specific information such as the specific date or exact magnitude of a phenomenon. It may also include approximate or relative information such as an approximate time period or the general order of magnitude of a phenomenon.

> The recall of major facts about particular cultures.
> The possession of a minimum knowledge about the organisms studied in the laboratory.

1.20   Knowledge of Ways and Means of Dealing
          with Specifics

Knowledge of the ways of organizing, studying, judging, and criticizing. This includes the methods of inquiry, the chronological sequences, and the standards of judgment within a field as well as the patterns of organization through which

---

[2] Each subcategory is followed by illustrative educational objectives selected from the literature.

the areas of the fields themselves are determined and internally organized. This knowledge is at an intermediate level of abstraction between specific knowledge on the one hand and knowledge of universals on the other. It does not so much demand the activity of the student in using the materials as it does a more passive awareness of their nature.

1.21 Knowledge of Conventions. Knowledge of characteristic ways of treating and presenting ideas and phenomena. For purposes of communication and consistency, workers in a field employ usages, styles, practices, and forms that best suit their purposes and/or that appear to suit best the phenomena with which they deal. It should be recognized that although these forms and conventions are likely to be set up on arbitrary, accidental, or authoritative bases, they are retained because of the general agreement or concurrence of individuals concerned with the subject, phenomena, or problem.

> Familiarity with the forms and conventions of the major types of works; e.g., verse, plays, scientific papers, etc.
>
> To make pupils conscious of correct form and usage in speech and writing.

1.22 Knowledge of Trends and Sequences. Knowledge of the processes, directions, and movements of phenomena with respect to time.

> Understanding of the continuity and development of American culture as exemplified in American life.
>
> Knowledge of the basic trends underlying the development of public assistance programs.

1.23 Knowledge of Classifications and Categories. Knowledge of the classes, sets, divisions, and arrangements that are regarded as fundamental for a given subject field, purpose, argument, or problem.

> To recognize the area encompassed by various kinds of problems or materials.
>
> Becoming familiar with a range of types of literature.

1.24 Knowledge of Criteria. Knowledge of the criteria by which facts, principles, opinions, and conduct are tested or judged.

> Familiarity with criteria for judgment appropriate to the type of work and the purpose for which it is read.
>
> Knowledge of criteria for the evaluation of recreational activities.

1.25 Knowledge of Methodology. Knowledge of the methods of inquiry, techniques, and procedures employed in a particular subject field as well as those employed in investigating particular problems and phenomena. The emphasis here is on the individual's knowledge of the method rather than his ability to use the method.

> Knowledge of scientific methods for evaluating health concepts.
>
> The student shall know the methods of attack relevant to the kinds of problems of concern to the social sciences.

1.30 Knowledge of the Universals and Abstractions in a Field.

Knowledge of the major schemes and patterns by which phenomena and ideas are organized. These are the large structures, theories, and generalizations that dominate a subject field or that are quite generally used in studying phenomena or solving problems. These are at the highest levels of abstraction and complexity.

1.31 Knowledge of Principles and Generalizations. Knowledge of particular abstractions that summarize observations of phenomena. These are the abstractions that are of value in explaining, describing, predicting, or determining the most appropriate and relevant action or direction to be taken.

> Knowledge of the important principles by which our experience with biological phenomena is summarized.
>
> The recall of major generalizations about particular cultures.

1.32 Knowledge of Theories and Structures. Knowledge of the *body* of principles and generalizations together with their interrelations that present a clear, rounded, and systematic view of a complex phenomenon, problem, or field. These are the most abstract formulations, and they can be used to show the interrelation and organization of a great range of specifics.

> The recall of major theories about particular cultures.
>
> Knowledge of a relatively complete formulation of the theory of evolution.

Intellectual Abilities and Skills

Abilities and skills refer to organized modes of operation and generalized techniques for dealing with materials and problems. The materials and problems may be of such a nature that little or no specialized and technical information is required. Such information as is required can be assumed to be part of the individual's general fund of knowledge. Other problems may require specialized and technical information at a rather high level such that specific knowledge and skill in dealing with the problem and the materials are required. The abilities and skills objectives emphasize the mental processes of organizing and reorganizing material to achieve a particular purpose. The materials may be given or remembered.

2.00 COMPREHENSION

This represents the lowest level of understanding. It refers to a type of understanding or apprehension such that the individual knows what is being communicated and can make use of the material or idea being communicated without necessarily relating it to other material or seeing its fullest implications.

2.10 Translation

Comprehension as evidenced by the care and accuracy with which the communication is paraphrased or rendered from one language or form of communication to another. Translation is judged on the basis of faithfulness and accuracy; that is, on the extent to which the material in the original communication is preserved although the form of the communication has been altered.

> The ability to understand nonliteral statements (metaphor, symbolism, irony, exaggeration).
>
> Skill in translating mathematical verbal material into symbolic statements and vice versa.

2.20 Interpretation

The explanation or summarization of a communication. Whereas translation involves an objective part-for-part rendering of a communication, interpretation involves a reordering, rearrangement, or new view of the material.

> The ability to grasp the thought of the work as a whole at any desired level of generality.
>
> The ability to interpret various types of social data.

2.30   Extrapolation

The extension of trends or tendencies beyond the given data to determine implications, consequences, corollaries, effects, etc., in accordance with the conditions described in the original communication.

The ability to deal with the conclusions of a work in terms of the immediate inference made from the explicit statements.

Skill in predicting continuation of trends.

3.00   APPLICATION

The use of abstractions in particular and concrete situations. The abstractions may be in the form of general ideas, rules of procedures, or generalized methods. The abstractions may also be technical principles, ideas, and theories that must be remembered and applied.

Application to the phenomena discussed in one paper of the scientific terms or concepts used in other papers.

The ability to predict the probable effect of a change in a factor on a biological situation previously at equilibrium.

4.00   ANALYSIS

The breakdown of a communication into its constituent elements or parts such that the relative hierarchy of ideas is made clear and/or the relations between the ideas expressed are made explicit. Such analyses are intended to clarify the communication, to indicate how the communication is organized, and the way in which it manages to convey its effects, as well as its basis and arrangement.

4.10   Analysis of Elements

Identification of the elements included in a communication.

The ability to recognize unstated assumptions.

Skill in distinguishing facts from hypotheses.

4.20   Analysis of Relationships

The connections and interactions between elements and parts of a communication.

Ability to check the consistency of hypotheses with given information and assumptions.

Skill in comprehending the interrelationships among the ideas in a passage.

4.30   Analysis of Organizational Principles

The organization, systematic arrangement, and structure that hold the communication together. This includes the "explicit" as well as "implicit" structure. It includes the bases, necessary arrangement, and mechanics that make the communication a unit.

> The ability to recognize form and pattern in literary or artistic works as a means of understanding their meaning.
>
> Ability to recognize the general techniques used in persuasive materials such as advertising, propaganda, etc.

5.00   SYNTHESIS

The putting together of elements and parts so as to form a whole. This involves the process of working with pieces, parts, elements, etc., and arranging and combining them in such a way as to constitute a pattern or structure not clearly there before.

5.10   Production of a Unique Communication

The development of a communication in which the writer or speaker attempts to convey ideas, feelings, and/or experiences to others.

> Skill in writing, using an excellent organization of ideas and statements.
>
> Ability to tell a personal experience effectively.

5.20   Production of a Plan or Proposed Set of Operations

The development of a plan of work or the proposal of a plan of operations. The plan should satisfy requirements of the task that may be given to the student or that he may develop for himself.

> Ability to propose ways of testing hypotheses.
>
> Ability to plan a unit of instruction for a particular teaching situation.

5.30   Derivation of a Set of Abstract Relations

The development of a set of abstract relations either to classify or explain particular data or phenomena, or the deduction of propositions and relations from a set of basic propositions or symbolic representations.

Ability to formulate appropriate hypotheses based upon an analysis of factors involved, and to modify such hypotheses in the light of new factors and considerations.

Ability to make mathematical discoveries and generalizations.

6.00 EVALUATION

Judgments about the value of material and methods for given purposes. Quantitative and qualitative judgments about the extent to which material and methods satisfy criteria. Use of a standard of appraisal. The criteria may be those determined by the student or those given to him.

6.10 Judgments in Terms of Internal Evidence

Evaluation of the accuracy of a communication from such evidence as logical accuracy, consistency, and other internal criteria.

Judging by internal standards, the ability to assess general probability of accuracy in reporting facts from the care given to exactness of statement, documentation, proof, etc.

The ability to indicate logical fallacies in arguments.

6.20 Judgments in Terms of External Criteria

Evaluation of material with reference to selected or remembered criteria.

The comparison of major theories, generalizations, and facts about particular cultures.

Judging by external standards, the ability to compare a work with the highest known standards in its field—especially with other works of recognized excellence.

Affective Domain

The second largest number of objectives found in the educational literature could be placed into one of the levels of the affective domain. The taxonomy committee found it more difficult to determine a hierarchal order of affective behaviors. The affective domain contains behaviors and objectives that have some emotional overtone. It encompasses likes and dislikes, attitudes, values, and beliefs. The following is an abstract of the taxonomy of educational objectives for the affective domain.

A Condensed Version of the Affective Domain of the Taxonomy of Educational Objectives[3]

1.0   RECEIVING (ATTENDING)

At this level we are concerned that the learner be sensitized to the existence of certain phenomena and stimuli, that is, be willing to receive or to attend to them. This is clearly the first and crucial step if the learner is to be properly oriented to learn what the teacher intends to be learned. To indicate that this is the bottom rung of the ladder, however, is not at all to imply that the teacher is starting *de novo*. Because of previous experience (formal or informal), the student brings to each situation a point of view or set that may facilitate or hinder recognition of the phenomena to which the teacher is trying to provide sensitivity.

The category of *Receiving* has been divided into three subcategories to indicate three different levels of attending to phenomena. While the division points between the subcategories are arbitrary, the subcategories do represent a continuum. From an extremely passive position or role on the part of the learner, where the sole responsibility for the evocation of the behavior rests with the teacher—that is, the responsibility entails "capturing" the student's attention—the continuum extends to a point at which the learner directs attention, at least at a semiconscious level, toward the preferred stimuli.

1.1   Awareness

Awareness is almost a cognitive behavior. But unlike *Knowledge*, the lowest level of the cognitive domain, we are not so much concerned with a memory of, or ability to recall, an item or fact as we are that, given appropriate opportunity, the learner will merely be conscious of something—that account be taken of a situation, phenomenon, object, or state of affairs. Like *Knowledge* it does imply an assessment of the qualities or nature of the stimulus, but unlike *Knowledge* it does not

---

[3] From David R. Krathwohl, Benjamin S. Bloom, and Bertram B. Masia, *Taxonomy of Educational Objectives—The Classification of Educational Goals, Handbook II: Affective Domain.* New York: David McKay Co., Inc., © 1964, pp. 176–185. Reprinted by permission of David McKay Co., Inc.

necessarily imply attention. There can be simple awareness without specific discrimination or recognition of the objective characteristics of the object, even though these characteristics must be deemed to have an effect. The individual may not be able to verbalize the aspects of the stimulus that cause the awareness.

> Develops awareness of aesthetic factors in dress, furnishings, architecture, city design, good art, and the like.
>
> Develops some consciousness of color, form, arrangement, and design in the objects and structures in the environment and in descriptive or symbolic representations of people, things, and situations.[4]

1.2 Willingness to Receive

In this category we have come a step up the ladder but are still dealing with what appears to be cognitive behavior. At a minimum level, we are here describing the behavior of being willing to tolerate a given stimulus, not to avoid it. Like *Awareness*, it involves a neutrality or suspended judgment toward the stimulus. At this level of the continuum the teacher is not concerned that the student seek it out, nor even, perhaps, that in an environment crowded with many other stimuli the learner will necessarily attend to the stimulus. Rather, at worst, given the opportunity to attend in a field with relatively few competing stimuli, the learner is not actively seeking to avoid it. At best, one is willing to take notice of the phenomenon and give it attention.

> Attends (carefully) when others speak—in direct conversation, on the telephone, in audiences.
>
> Appreciation (tolerance) of cultural patterns exhibited by individuals from other groups—religious, social, political, economic, national, etc.
>
> Increase in sensitivity to human need and pressing social problems.

1.3 Controlled or Selected Attention

At a somewhat higher level we are concerned with a new phenomenon, the differentiation of a given stimulus into figure

---

[4] Illustrative objectives selected from the literature follow the description of each subcategory.

and ground at a conscious or perhaps semiconscious level—the differentiation of aspects of a stimulus that is perceived as clearly marked off from adjacent impressions. The perception is still without tension or assessment, and the student may not know the technical terms of symbols with which to describe it correctly or precisely to others. In some instances it may refer not so much to the selectivity of attention as to the control of attention, so that when certain stimuli are present they will be attended to. There is an element of the learner's controlling the attention here, so that the favored stimulus is selected and attended to despite competing and distracting stimuli.

> Listens to music with some discrimination as to its mood and meaning and with some recognition of the contributions of various musical elements and instruments to the total effect.
>
> Alertness toward human values and judgments on life as they are recorded in literature.

2.0 RESPONDING

At this level we are concerned with responses that go beyond merely attending to the phenomenon. The student is sufficiently motivated as to not just be 1.2 *Willing to attend,* but perhaps to be actively attending. As a first stage in a "learning by doing" process the student is becoming committed in some small measure to the phenomena involved. This is a very low level of commitment, and we would not say at this level that this was "a personal value" or that one had "such and such an attitude." These terms belong to the next higher level that we describe. But we could say that one is doing something with or about the phenomenon besides merely perceiving it, as would be true at the next level below this of 1.3 *Controlled or selected attention.*

This is the category that many teachers will find best describes their "interest" objectives. Most commonly we use the term to indicate the desire that a child become sufficiently involved in or committed to a subject, phenomenon, or activity so as to seek it out and gain satisfaction from working with it or engaging in it.

2.1 Acquiescence in Responding

We might use the word "obedience" or "compliance" to describe this behavior. As both of these terms indicate, there is a passiveness so far as the initiation of the behavior is concerned, and the stimulus calling for this behavior is not subtle. Compliance is perhaps a better term than obedience, since there is more of the element of reaction to a suggestion and less of the implication of resistance or yielding unwillingly. The student makes the response, without fully accepting the necessity for doing so.

> Willingness to comply with health regulations.
> Obeys the playground regulations.

2.2 Willingness to Respond

The key to this level is in the term "willingness," with its implication of capacity for voluntary activity. There is the implication that the learner is sufficiently committed to exhibiting the behavior not just because of a fear of punishment, but "on one's own" or voluntarily. It may help to note that the element of resistance or of yielding unwillingly, which is possibly present at the previous level, is here replaced with consent or proceeding from one's own choice.

> Acquaints oneself with significant current issues in international, political, social, and economic affairs through voluntary reading and discussion.
>
> Acceptance of responsibility for personal health and for the protection of the health of others.

2.3 Satisfaction in Response

The additional element in the step beyond the *Willingness to respond* level, the consent, the assent to responding, or the voluntary response, is that the behavior is accompanied by a feeling of satisfaction, an emotional response, generally of pleasure, zest, or enjoyment. The location of this category in the hierarchy has given us a great deal of difficulty. Just where in the process of internalization that attachment of an emotional response, kick, or thrill to a behavior occurs has been hard to determine. For that matter there is some uncertainty as to whether the level of internalization at which it occurs may not depend on the particular behavior. We have even questioned whether it should be a category. If our structure is to be a hierarchy, then each category should include the behavior in the next level below it. The emotional component appears gradually through the range of internalization categories. The attempt to specify a given position in the hierarchy as *the* one at which the emotional component is added is doomed to failure.

The category is arbitrarily placed at this point in the hierarchy where it seems to appear most frequently and where it is cited as, or appears to be, an important component of the objectives at this level on the continuum. The category's inclusion at this point serves the pragmatic purpose of reminding us of the presence of the emotional component and its value in the building of affective behaviors. But it should not be thought of as appearing and occurring at this one point in the continuum and thus destroying the hierarchy that we are attempting to build.

> Enjoyment of self-expression in music and in arts and crafts as another means of personal enrichment.
>
> Finds pleasure in reading for recreation.
>
> Takes pleasure in conversing with many different kinds of people.

3.0 VALUING

This is the only category headed by a term that is in common use in the expression of objectives by teachers. Further, it is employed in its usual sense: that a thing, phenomenon, or behavior has worth. This abstract concept of worth is in part a result of the individual's own valuing or assessment, but it is much more a social product that has been slowly internalized or accepted and has come to be used by the student as a personal criterion of worth.

Behavior categorized at this level is sufficiently consistent and stable to have taken on the characteristics of a belief or an attitude. The learner displays this behavior with sufficient consistency in appropriate situations so as to be perceived as holding a value. At this level we are not concerned with the relationships among values but rather with the internalization of a set of specified, ideal values. Viewed from another standpoint, the objectives classified here are the prime stuff from which the conscience of the individual is developed into active control of behavior.

This category will be found appropriate for many objectives that use the term "attitude" (as well as, of course, "value").

An important element of behavior characterized by *Valuing* is that it is motivated, not by the desire to comply or obey, but by the individual's commitment to the underlying value guiding the behavior.

3.1 Acceptance of a Value

At this level we are concerned with the ascribing of worth to a phenomenon, behavior, object, etc. The term "belief," which is defined as "the emotional acceptance of a proposition or doctrine upon what one implicitly considers adequate ground" (English and English, 1958, p. 64), describes quite well what may be thought of as the dominant characteristic here. Beliefs have varying degrees of certitude. At this lowest level of *Valuing* we are concerned with the lowest levels of certainty; that is, there is more a readiness to reevaluate one's position than at the higher levels. It is a position that is somewhat tentative.

One of the distinguishing characteristics of this behavior is consistency of response to the class of objects, phenomena, etc., with which the belief or attitude is identified. It is consistent enough so that the person is perceived by others as holding the belief or value. At the level we are describing here, one is both sufficiently consistent that others can identify the value and sufficiently committed so as to be willing to be so identified.

> Continuing desire to develop the ability to speak and write effectively.
>
> Grows in own sense of kinship with human beings of all nations.

3.2 Preference for a Value

The provision for this subdivision arose out of a feeling that there were objectives that expressed a level of internalization between the mere acceptance of a value and commitment or conviction in the usual connotation of deep involvement in an area. Behavior at this level implies not just the acceptance of a value to the point of being willing to be identified with it, but the individual is sufficiently committed to the value to pursue it, to seek it out, and to want it.

> Assumes responsibility for drawing reticent members of a group into conversation.
>
> Deliberately examines a variety of viewpoints on controversial issues with a view to forming opinions about them.
>
> Actively participates in arranging for the showing of contemporary artistic efforts.

3.3 Commitment

Belief at this level involves a high degree of certainty. The ideas of "conviction" and "certainty beyond a shadow of a doubt" help to convey further the level of behavior intended. In some instances this may border on faith, in the sense of it being a firm emotional acceptance of a belief upon admittedly non-rational grounds. Loyalty to a position, group, or cause would also be classified here.

The person who displays behavior at this level is clearly perceived as holding the value. One acts to further the thing valued in some way, to extend the possibility of developing it, to deepen personal involvement with it and with the things representing it. One tries to convince others and seeks converts to the cause. There is a tension here that needs to be satisfied; action is the result of an aroused need or drive. There is a real motivation to act out the behavior.

> Devotion to those ideas and ideals that are the foundations of democracy.

> Faith in the power of reason and in methods of experiment and discussion.

4.0 ORGANIZATION

As the learner successively internalizes values, he or she encounters situations for which more than one value is relevant. Thus necessity arises for: a) the organization of the values into a system, b) the determination of the interrelationships among them, and c) the establishment of the dominant and pervasive ones. Such a system is built gradually, subject to change as new values are incorporated. This category is intended as the proper classification for objectives that describe the beginnings of the building of a value system. It is subdivided into two levels, since a prerequisite to interrelating is the conceptualization of the value in a form that permits organization. *Conceptualization* forms the first subdivision in the organization process, *Organization of a value system* the second.

While the order of the two subcategories seems appropriate enough with reference to one another, it is not so certain that 4.1 *Conceptualization of a value* is properly placed as the next level above 3.3 *Commitment*. Conceptualization undoubtedly begins at an earlier level for some objectives. Like 2.3 *Satis-*

faction in response, it is doubtful that a single completely satisfactory location for this category can be found. Positioning it before 4.2 *Organization of a value system* appropriately indicates a prerequisite of such a system. It also calls attention to a component of affective growth that occurs at least by this point on the continuum but may begin earlier.

4.1 Conceptualization of a Value

In the previous category, 3.0 *Valuing*, we noted that consistency and stability are integral characteristics of the particular value or belief. At this level (4.1) the quality of abstraction or conceptualization is added. This permits the individual to see how the value relates to those already held or to new ones that are coming to be held.

Conceptualization will be abstract, and in this sense it will be symbolic. But the symbols need not be verbal symbols. Whether conceptualization first appears at this point on the affective continuum is a moot point, as noted above.

Attempts to identify the characteristics of an admired art object.

Forms judgments as to the responsibility of society for conserving human and material resources.

4.2 Organization of a Value System

Objectives properly classified here are those that require the learner to bring together a complex of values, possibly disparate values, and to bring these into an ordered relationship with one another. Ideally, the ordered relationship will be one that is harmonious and internally consistent. This is, of course, the goal of such objectives, which seek to have the student formulate a philosophy of life. In actuality, the integration may be something less than entirely harmonious. More likely the relationship is better described as a kind of dynamic equilibrium that is, in part, dependent upon those portions of the environment that are salient at any point in time. In many instances the organization of values may result in their synthesis into a new value or value complex of a higher order.

Weighs alternative social policies and practices against the standards of the public welfare rather than the advantage of specialized and narrow interest groups.

Develops a plan for regulating rest in accordance with the demands of his or her activities.

5.0 CHARACTERIZATION BY A VALUE OR VALUE COMPLEX

At this level of internalization the values already have a place in the individual's value hierarchy; are organized into some kind of internally consistent system; have controlled the behavior of the individual for a sufficient time that adaptation has been made to behaving this way; and an evocation of the behavior no longer arouses emotion or affect except when the individual is threatened or challenged.

The individual acts consistently in accordance with the values internalized at this level, and our concern is to indicate two things: a) the generalization of this control to so much of the individual's behavior that one can describe and characterize the person by these pervasive controlling tendencies, and b) the integration of these beliefs, ideas, and attitudes into a total philosophy or world view. These two aspects constitute the subcategories.

5.1 Generalized Set

The generalized set is that which gives an internal consistency to the system of attitudes and values at any particular moment. It is selective responding at a very high level. It is sometimes spoken of as a determining tendency, an orientation toward phenomena, or a predisposition to act in a certain way. The generalized set is a response to highly generalized phenomena. It is a persistent and consistent response to a family of related situations or objects. It may often be an unconscious set that guides action without conscious forethought. The generalized set may be thought of as closely related to the idea of an attitude cluster, where the commonality is based on behavioral characteristics rather than the subject or object of the attitude. A generalized set is a basic orientation that enables the individual to reduce and order the complex world within one's environment and to act consistently and effectively in it.

> Readiness to revise judgments and to change behavior in the light of evidence.
>
> Judges problems and issues in terms of situations, issues, purposes, and consequences involved rather than in terms of fixed, dogmatic precepts or emotional wishful thinking.

5.2 Characterization

This, the peak of the internalization process, includes those objectives that are broadest with respect both to the phenomena covered and to the range of behavior that they comprise. Thus, here are found those objectives that concern one's view of the universe, one's philosophy of life, one's *Weltanschauung*—a value system having as its object the whole of what is known or knowable.

Objectives categorized here are more than generalized sets in the sense that they involve a greater inclusiveness and, within the group of attitudes, behaviors, beliefs, or ideas, an emphasis on internal consistency. Though this internal consistency may not always be exhibited behaviorally by the students toward whom the objective is directed, since we are categorizing teachers' objectives, this consistency feature will always be a component of *Characterization* objectives.

As the title of the category implies, these objectives are so encompassing that they tend to characterize the individual almost completely.

> Develops for regulation of one's personal and civic life a code of behavior based on ethical principles consistent with democratic ideals.
> Develops a consistent philosophy of life.

Psychomotor Domain

Bloom's committee did not develop a taxonomy for the psychomotor domain. Moreover, until recently little work had been done in this area. Below is an example of one of the more recent developments in the construction of a taxonomy for behaviors in the psychomotor domain.

——————— *Branching Option Three* ———————

At this point you may find it beneficial to turn to Appendix C. There you will find a brief article designed to show you how specific objectives may be formulated within the hierarchy of the major levels and sublevels of the taxonomies of educational objectives as set forth by Bloom et al. (1956) and Krathwohl et al. (1964).

The Classification of Educational Objectives in the Psychomotor Domain[5]

The major organizational principle operating is that of complexity with attention to the sequence involved in the performance of a motor act. That is, objectives that would be classified at the lower levels are less complex in nature than related objectives at upper levels. In general, they are easier to carry out. And, those at the upper levels build on those at the lower. Harrow's [1972] taxonomy for the psychomotor domain is useful for classifying when a variety of skills need to be learned and mastered.)

1.00 PERCEPTION

This is an essential first step in performing a motor act. It is the process of becoming aware of objects, qualities, or relations by way of the sense organs. It is a necessary but not sufficient condition for motor activity. It is basic in the situation-interpretation-action chain leading to motor activity. The category of perception has been divided into three subcategories indicating three different levels of the perception process. This level is a parallel of the first category, receiving or attending, in the affective domain.

1.10 Sensory Stimulation
Impingement of a stimulus upon one or more of the sense organs.

1.11 Auditory. Hearing or the sense of organs of hearing.

1.12 Visual. Concerned with the mental pictures or images obtained through the eyes.

1.13 Tactile. Pertaining to the sense of touch.

1.14 Taste. Determine the relish or flavor by taking a portion into the mouth.

1.15 Smell. To perceive by excitation of the olfactory nerves.

---

[5] From Elizabeth Jane Simpson, "The Classification of Educational Objectives in the Psychomotor Domain," *Illinois Teacher of Home Economics* 10, 1966-1967, 135-141.

1.16 Kinesthetic. The muscle sense; pertaining to sensitivity from activation of receptors in muscles, tendons, and joints.

1.10 Sensory Stimulation—Illustrative educational objectives.

> Sensitivity to auditory cues in playing a musical instrument as a member of a group.
> Awareness of difference in "hand" of various fabrics.
> Sensitivity to flavors in seasoning food.

The preceding categories are not presented in any special order of importance, although, in Western cultures, the visual cues are said to have dominance, whereas in some cultures, the auditory and tactile cues may preempt the high position we give the visual. Probably no sensible ordering of these is possible at this time. It should also be pointed out that "the cues that guide action may change for a particular motor activity as learning progresses (e.g., kinesthetic cues replacing visual cues)."[6]

1.20 CUE SELECTION

Deciding to what cues one must respond in order to satisfy the particular requirements of task performance. This involves identification of the cue or cues and associating them with the task to be performed.

It may involve grouping of cues in terms of past experience and knowledge. Cues relevant to the situation are selected as a guide to action; irrelevant cues are ignored or discarded.

1.20 Cue Selection—Illustrative educational objectives.

> Recognition of operating difficulties with machinery through the sound of the machine in operation.
> Sensing where the needle should be set in beginning machine stitching.
> Recognizing factors to take into account in batting in a softball game.

1.30 Translation

Relating of perception to action in performing a motor act. This is the mental process of determining the meaning of the cues received for action. It involves symbolic translation, that is, having an image or being reminded of something,

---

[6] Ray Loree, correspondence with investigator, June 1965.

"having an idea," as a result of cues received. It may involve insight that is essential in solving a problem through perceiving the relationships essential to solution. Sensory translation is an aspect of this level. It involves "feedback," that is, knowledge of the effects of the process. Translation is a continuous part of the motor act being performed.

1.30   Translation—Illustrative educational objectives.

Ability to relate music to dance form.

Ability to follow a recipe in preparing food.

Knowledge of the "feel" of operating a sewing machine successfully and use of this knowledge as a guide in stitching.

2.00   SET

Set is a preparatory adjustment of readiness for a particular kind of action or experience.

Three aspects of set have been identified: mental, physical, and emotional.

2.10   Mental Set

Readiness, in the mental sense, to perform a certain motor act. This involves, as prerequisite, the level of perception and its subcategories. Discrimination, that is, using judgment in making distinctions, is an aspect of mental set.

2.10   Mental set—Illustrative educational objectives.

Knowledge of steps in setting the table.

Knowledge of tools appropriate for performance of various sewing operations.

2.20   Physical Set

Readiness in the sense of having made the anatomical adjustments necessary for a motor act to be performed. Readiness, in the physical sense, involves receptor set, that is, sensory attending, or focusing the attention of the needed sensory organs and postural set, or positioning of the body.

2.20   Physical   set—Illustrative   educational   objectives.

Achievement of bodily stance preparatory to bowling.

Positioning of hands preparatory to typing.

2.30   Emotional Set

Readiness in terms of attitudes favorable to the motor acts taking place. Willingness to respond is implied.

2.30 Emotional set—Illustrative educational objectives.

Disposition to perform sewing machine operation to best of ability.
Desire to operate a production drill press with skill.

3.00 GUIDED RESPONSE

This is an early step in the development of skill. Emphasis here is upon the abilities that are components of the more complex skill. Guided response is the overt behavioral act of an individual under the guidance of the instructor or in response to self-evaluation where the student has a model or criteria against which to judge personal performance. Prerequisites to performance of the act are readiness to respond, in terms of set to produce the overt behavioral act and selection of the appropriate response. Selection of response may be defined as deciding what response must be made in order to satisfy the requirements of task performance. There appear to be two major subcategories, imitation and trial and error.

3.10 Imitation
Imitation is the execution of an act as a direct response to the perception of another person performing the act.

3.10 Imitation—Illustrative educational objectives.

Imitation of the process of stay-stitching the curved neck edge of a bodice.
Performing a dance step as demonstrated.
Debeaking a chick in the manner demonstrated.

3.20 Trial and Error
Trying various responses, usually with some rationale for each response, until an appropriate response is achieved. The appropriate response is one that meets the requirements of task performance, that is, "gets the job done" or does it more efficiently. This level may be defined as multiple-response learning in which the proper response is selected out of varied behaviors, possibly through the influence of reward and punishment.

3.20 Trial and error—Illustrative educational objectives.

Discovering the most efficient method of ironing a blouse through trial of various procedures.
Determining the sequence for cleaning a room through trial of several patterns.

4.00 MECHANISM

Learned response has become habitual. At this level the learner has achieved a certain confidence and degree of proficiency in the performance of the act. The act is a part of one's repertoire of possible responses to stimuli and the demands of situations where the response is an appropriate one. The response may be more complex than at the preceding level; it may involve some patterning in carrying out the task.

4.00 Mechanism—Illustrative educational objectives.

Ability to perform a hand-hemming operation.
Ability to mix ingredients for butter cake.
Ability to pollinate an oat flower.

5.00 COMPLEX OVERT RESPONSE

At this level the individual can perform a motor act that is considered complex because of the movement pattern required. At this level skill has been attained. The act can be carried out smoothly and efficiently, that is, with minimum expenditure of time and energy. There are two subcategories: resolution of uncertainty and automatic performance.

5.10 Resolution of Uncertainty

The act is performed without hesitation of the individual to get a mental picture of task sequence. That is, one knows the sequence required and so proceeds with confidence. The act is here defined as complex in nature.

5.10 Resolution of uncertainty—Illustrative educational objectives.

Skill in operating a milling machine.
Skill in setting up and operating a production band saw.

5.20 Automatic Performance

At this level the individual can perform a finely coordinated motor skill with a great deal of ease and muscle control.

5.20 Automatic performance—Illustrative educational objectives.

Skill in performing basic steps of national folk dances.
Skill in tailoring a suit.
Skill in performing on the violin.

6.00   ADAPTATION

Altering motor activities to meet the demands of new problematic situations requiring a physical response.

6.00   Adaptation—Illustrative educational objectives.

Developing a modern dance composition through adapting known abilities and skills in dance.

7.00   ORIGINATION

Creating new motor acts or ways of manipulating materials out of understandings, abilities, and skills developed in the psychomotor area.

7.00   Origination—Illustrative educational objectives.

Creation of a modern dance.

Creation of a new game requiring psychomotor response.

Implementing Behavioral Taxonomies

Now that we have examined these taxonomies, you should practice using them to classify instructional objectives. You might try the following strategy in learning how to employ the taxonomies. First, turn to Appendix A in the text. There you will find several instructional objectives from various subject areas. Select several of the objectives listed and try to classify them using the three taxonomies. Remember that in doing so you must make two decisions: 1) the kind of learning outcome described in the objective (i.e., cognitive, affective, psychomotor), and 2) the level of the behavior implied by the objective within a particular domain.

When you have had sufficient practice in making these discriminations you may want to expand your skills in a slightly different direction. Select a unit of instruction from your own subject area. Develop a list of general objectives that describe the behaviors you want learners to demonstrate during and after the instructional unit. Now, examine each objective carefully and use the taxonomies to classify each one as you did for the objectives in Appendix A. You might use the synthesized version of the taxonomies contained in Appendix C as a flow chart for recording how each objective is classified.

How does your instructional unit look? Do you have an adequate sampling of desired types of learning outcomes or does your flow chart appear to be leaning toward a particular type of outcome? Note that the latter finding is not necessarily undesirable. It may be that you have selected a unit of instruction that is predominantly in one domain of behavior. In any case, the classification of objectives should reveal the relative distribution of the kind of learning outcomes dealt with in your objectives. This information should be valuable to you in assessing the extent to which current unit objectives reflect the kind of learner outcomes that you want students to achieve.

Now, examine the distribution of objectives within a particular domain. Have you focused your objectives on lower-level learning outcomes or do you have a relatively even distribution across various levels? Again, there is no inherent positive/negative assessment that can be made on the basis of the distribution alone. You must assess the distribution in light of what are the important types (i.e., levels) of learning outcomes relevant to your particular instructional unit. It may be that the particular unit selected is one that should focus on baseline, low-level behaviors as opposed to more complex forms of behavior. On the other hand, such a distribution for another kind of unit may suggest that you have devoted too much time to low-level behaviors and need to develop objectives that describe more complex behaviors.

Often teachers find that an analysis of learning outcomes is quite revealing. Sometimes we assume that our approach to a particular instructional unit is accomplishing desired goals, when in fact we are not achieving the level of sophistication that we really want in our students. An analysis of learning outcomes in the manner suggested can provide valuable information about the kind and level of learning outcomes in any size unit of instruction.

An Aid to the Sequencing of Instructional Objectives

So far in this chapter we have emphasized the role of behavioral taxonomies in aiding one to write and classify instructional objectives. Among the advantages of classifying objectives is that it helps to identify the general structure of a given unit of instruction in terms of the kinds and levels of relevant learning outcomes stated in objectives. While this is an important and useful phase in the employment of instructional objectives, there are additional aspects related to their implementation that should be considered.

Once objectives are written and classified, they must be sequenced in a manner to enhance learning. A careful taxonomic classification of instructional objectives may provide excellent direction for how they may be sequenced. The classification of objectives according to behavioral taxonomies provides a general overview of the kinds and types of learning outcomes that are desired for a particular unit of instruction. While this is useful, more specific information is needed about desired learning outcomes in order to plan and sequence instruction. For example, consider the teacher who is in the process of developing a unit of instruction on public speaking. In following our suggestions, the teacher has listed the general objectives desirable for learners to achieve during and at the end of the unit of instruction. In addition, these objectives have been classified according to some category scheme, namely the traditional three-category system. The classification of objectives in the cognitive domain looks something like this:

GENERAL UNIT OBJECTIVE: *Students should be able to speak effectively in public.*

Instructional Objectives for the Cognitive Domain

Taxonomy Classification	*Objective*
Knowledge:	
of terminology (1.11)	Able to distinguish among various types of speeches and their function.
	Able to distinguish among various parts of a speech and their function.
	Able to recall specific facts for use in speech development.
of conventions (1.21)	Able to use accepted forms of language in a speech.
	Able to identify standard ways of organizing speeches.
	Able to select an appropriate form of visual aid.

of criteria (1.24)	Able to identify the major criteria used by professionals in assessing a speech. Able to identify criteria for testing the validity of evidence.
of methodology (1.25)	Able to identify methods for analyzing an audience. Able to recall techniques for acquiring evidence and supporting materials.
of theories and structures (1.32)	Able to recall major rhetorical theories.

Comprehension:
translation (2.10)   Able to illustrate arguments using statistical evidence.
                            Able to represent ideas through metaphors.
                            Able to restate ideas using different language forms.

interpretation (2.20)   Able to draw conclusions on the basis of evidence presented.

Application:
                            Able to organize ideas in a speech.
                            Able to choose evidence appropriate for a given audience.
                            Able to generalize conclusions based on evidence.

Analysis:
of elements (4.10)   Able to recognize unstable assumptions in a speech.
                            Able to categorize the arguments in a speech.
                            Able to identify the main points of a speech.

of relationships (4.20)   Able to distinguish fallacies in arguments.
                            Able to compare the validity of opposing arguments.

of organizational principles (4.30)   Able to distinguish forms of support.
                            Able to analyze the patterns of organization in a speech.
                            Able to analyze an audience.

Synthesis:
production of a unique communication (5.10)   Able to write a well organized speech.
                            Able to deliver a speech.

production of a plan or proposed set of operations (5.20)	Able to plan an outline of a speech. Able to plan a strategy for research a topic. Able to plan a strategy for audience analysis.
Evaluation: judgments in terms of internal evidence	Able to judge the effectiveness of a speech.

Examination of the classified objectives reveals a reasonably clear idea of what learning outcomes this teacher associates with the general objective "to be able to speak effectively in public." However, there is less information provided about how this teacher sequences the stated objectives in order to obtain the terminal objective of the unit. It is reasonable to assume that the teacher would begin instruction at the lower-level behaviors (e.g., knowledge, comprehension) and gradually work up to the higher-level behaviors (e.g., synthesis). Common sense, practical experience, and considerable research suggest that learners are able to master higher-level skills only when they have mastered prerequisite capabilities (see Gagné, 1977). Even if we are correct in the assumption that the teacher will begin instruction at the lower-level outcomes and work up to the higher-level outcomes, we still do not have enough information about how the sequencing of objectives is accomplished.

The objectives listed in the example are general in nature compared to the highly specific objectives illustrated in Chapter 3. Several of the objectives listed may require further breakdown into component competencies in order to understand how instruction may be sequenced. For example, consider this objective from the taxonomic classification list: *able to write a well organized speech.* This objective deals with a reasonably complex behavior that requires the learner to demonstrate several prerequisite skills. In order to determine how this general objective might be sequenced, it is necessary to assess what prerequisite skills are necessary to write a well organized speech. If the taxonomic classification of learning outcomes is extremely detailed, it may contain all of the prerequisite skills necessary to accomplish the general objective. However, most taxonomic classifications of objectives are not detailed enough to provide this information. It is only by breaking down the general objective into its component learning parts that the teacher is able to acquire a clear idea of how instruction might be sequenced to accomplish the objective.

The procedure for breaking down an objective into its component parts is called *task analysis*. The procedure is very useful for designing instruction that can be organized hierarchically; that is, where learning outcomes can be arranged according to subordinate and superordinate components. Careful task analysis can provide considerable direction in sequencing instruction to maximize learning efficiency and effectiveness (see Gagné, 1977).

Task analysis is by no means an easy procedure, although it is less difficult to conduct for some types of learning outcomes than for others (Gagné, 1977). The logic of the procedure is reasonably straightforward. Beginning with the terminal objective, one asks: what does a learner have to be able to do in order to accomplish that objective? The answer(s) to this question results in the identification of the necessary prerequiste skills that learners must have to achieve the terminal behavior. Presumably, these prerequisite skills in turn also have prerequisite skills that can be determined by again asking the central question. The key question is asked again and again until the answers are sufficient to assume that all learners possess the competencies necessary for instruction to begin. It is important to use action verbs (see Chapter 3) to describe each subordinate competency so that the analysis reflects observable behaviors. An example of a task analysis is provided in Figure 4-1.

The completed task analysis is useful for several reasons. First, it expands the taxonomic classification by providing detailed information about the specific components of each objective. Task analysis can be used "to fill in the gaps" of the general learning outcome analysis and to provide a more complete picture of the component parts (i.e., objectives) for a given unit of instruction. As can be seen in Figure 4-1, there are several additional objectives related to organizing a speech that were not included in the original list of learning outcomes. Imagine how much additional information could be added to the taxonomic classification objectives if a task analysis were completed on each of the complex objectives in the original list!

A second important use of task analysis is that it aids greatly in the sequencing of instruction. Task analysis provides

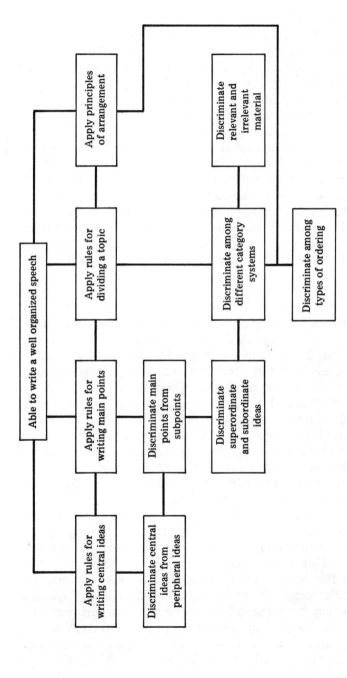

FIGURE 4-1. Task Analysis for a Complex Objective

See Haynes (1973) for more complete information on rules and concepts related to speech organization.

us with guidelines of the skills learners must possess before they can be expected to master superordinate competencies. Task analysis can be used to select and sequence objectives already included in the taxonomic classification, or to reveal objectives that must be added to the list. In either case, specific information is provided for sequencing objectives to maximize the efficiency and effectiveness of instruction.

Related to this advantage is the role of task analysis in selecting and developing instructional strategies. Research on various instructional strategies offers no conclusive findings about which instructional procedures are most effective for achieving given levels of learner outcomes. However, knowing the specific level of desired learner outcomes and how they are related provides a good basis for making intelligent decisions about the selection of instructional strategies. For example, concept and discrimination learning require different external learning conditions than rule or problem solving learning (Gagné, 1977). Instructional strategies used for achieving types of learning outcomes should reflect the basic differences in the nature of the learning task that is required. Task analysis helps us to identify various types of learning outcomes in terms of their hierarchical relationship and aids the educator in selecting instructional strategies that are particularly well suited for the kind of learning outcomes desired.

A fourth reason for using task analysis is related to evaluation, a major component of the instructional model. Breaking down a complex behavior into its component parts often provides considerable direction in selecting alternative ways of assessing learner achievement. For example, learners may be assessed throughout an instructional unit to determine where problems are encountered in mastering prerequisite skills. Such a procedure (often called *formative evaluation*) provides feedback to the teacher as well as students regarding where particular attention must be paid to the learning of necessary prerequisite skills. Often individualized instruction can be prescribed on the basis of such evaluation to deal with specific learning deficiencies. In addition, knowledge of the specific kind of learning outcomes and their relationships pertinent to a given unit of instruction provides essential information for final (i.e., summative) evaluation. For example, a common error in assessing student performance is to mismatch the level of behavior stated in the objective and the actual level of behavior evaluated (see Chapter 7). Sometimes a teacher will state a complex behavior in an objective and test students on simple recall and recognition, whereas at other times the mismatching is just the opposite. A task analysis (especially on complex objectives) helps to avoid this mismatching because clear guidelines are suggested for assessing various objectives in the hierarchy. Just as task analysis aids one in the selection of appropriate instructional strategies, it may also assist in designing hierarchically arranged assessment procedures.

Task analysis is also related to preassessment. Preassessment is designed to determine 1) whether students have the prerequisite behavioral capabilities for the instruction to follow, 2) how much of what is to be learned is already known, and 3) the instructional activities that should be presented to each student. Clearly, task analysis can provide essential information relevant to the design and implementation of preassessment procedures. It would appear extremely difficult to develop preassessment procedures without first doing some form of task analysis in order to break down complex objectives into component parts. More will be said about preassessment in the next chapter.

It should be clear by now that task analysis is a useful procedure in planning and implementing instructional decisions of various kinds. As such, the advantages of using a task analysis more than justify the time and effort required to develop it. Gagné (1977) is particularly helpful in discussing learning outcomes in terms of a hierarchical arrangement and offers useful suggestions and examples of task analysis. In addition, Gagné and Briggs (1974) offer suggestions for implementing other aspects of instruction that are based on task analysis procedures.

As you design an instructional unit in your field (i.e., the taxonomic classification done earlier), attempt to conduct a task analysis on several objectives in your list. This is perhaps one of the best ways to "get a feel" for using task analysis. You should be cautioned that it is a time-consuming procedure and that it takes some effort. However, once accomplished, you will likely see the many advantages the procedure offers for the design and implementation of instruction.

Summary

In this chapter we have focused on procedures for classifying and sequencing instructional objectives. It was suggested that a behavioral taxonomy is often useful as a classification scheme to organize instructional objectives. Taxonomies for the cognitive, affective, and psychomotor domains were presented. Suggestions were then offered for employing the taxonomies for classifying objectives.

Task analysis was examined as a procedure for sequencing objectives in a hierarchal arrangement. As such, task analysis is a procedure used to complement objective classification. Task analysis used in conjunction with taxonomic classification provides necessary information for sequencing instructional objectives.

REFERENCES

Bloom, B. S. (Ed.), Engelhart, N. D., Furst, E. J., Hill, W. H., and Krathwohl, D. R. *Taxonomy of educational objectives—the classification of educational goals, Handbook I: cognitive domain.* New York: David McKay Company, Inc., 1956.

Gagné, R. M. *The conditions of learning,* 3rd ed. New York: Holt, Rinehart and Winston, 1977.

_____. *Essentials of learning for instruction.* Hinsdale, Ill.: The Dryden Press, 1974.

Gagné, R. M., and Briggs, L. J. *Principles of instructional design.* New York: Holt, Rinehart and Winston, 1974.

Harrow, A. J. *A taxonomy of the psychomotor domain.* New York: David McKay Company, Inc., 1972.

Haynes, J. L. *Organizing a speech: a programmed guide.* Englewood Cliffs, N. J.: Prentice-Hall, Inc., 1973.

Krathwohl, D. R., Bloom, B. S., and Masia, B. B. *Taxonomy of educational goals, Handbook II: affective domain.* New York: David McKay Company, Inc., 1964.

Merrill, M. D. Necessary psychological conditions for defining instructional outcomes. *Educational Technology* 11, 1971, 34-39.

Seddon, G. M. The properties of Bloom's taxonomy of educational objectives for the cognitive domain. *Review of Educational Reserach* 48, 1978, 303-323.

Simpson, J. S. The classification of educational objectives in the psychomotor domain. *The Psychomotor Domain* 3, 1972, Gryphon House, 43–56.

Walbesser, H. H. An evaluation model and its application. Washington, D.C.: American Association for the Advancement of Science, 1965.

5

Preassessment and
Needs Assessment

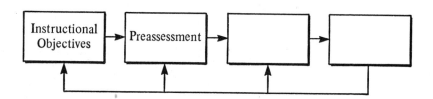

After completing this chapter, the learner should be able to:

1. State three reasons why preassessment of learners is conducted prior to beginning instruction;
2. State three types of information that the results of preassessment provide;
3. Distinguish between preassessment of entry behavior and preassessment of terminal behavior;
4. Describe a strategy for developing a preassessment test of entry and terminal behavior;
5. Distinguish between the terms *preassessment* and *needs assessment*;
6. List and describe four essential factors of a needs assessment;
7. Describe the classical technique of assessing needs;
8. Identify and explain the six models in the needs assessment taxonomy;

9. List nine methods of conducting needs assessment and explain their appropriate uses;
10. Describe five problems facing needs assessment and explain how they may be corrected in implementation.

The first part of this chapter is concerned with the second component of the general model of instruction, preassessment. In essence, preassessment involves evaluation of student performance, but it is different from typical evaluation procedures. Teachers most often use evaluation procedures for assessing students' performance at the end of a unit of instruction. Bloom, Hastings, and Madaus (1971) have referred to this type of assessment as *summative evaluation*. In our model, summative evaluation procedures would be used to assess students' mastery of instructional objectives *after* completing a unit of instruction (see Chapter 7). However, as the term implies, preassessment procedures are used to assess students' performance *before* instruction begins. We use the term pre*assessment* instead of pre*test* because the methods of measuring student performance include more than just written evaluations. Some skills are better measured by verbal expression or physical behavior (e.g., ability to recite the pledge of allegiance or ability in using sign language).

Just as it is important to identify student performance before instruction begins, it is also important for teachers to identify specific skills students will need in the future. Needs assessment is a technique that helps educators accomplish this goal. A properly conducted needs assessment benefits a school system by 1) increasing participation and communication among the administration, faculty, parents, and staff; 2) providing better information for decision making and planning; 3) giving specific feedback and evaluation; and 4) coordinating school operations more closely (Berrie, 1977). The second part of this chapter is concerned with the purposes, application, and prospects of needs assessment.

Preassessment

Preassessment of learners prior to beginning instruction is designed to determine: 1) whether learners have the prerequisite behavioral capabilities for the instruction to follow, 2) how much of what is to be learned is already known, and 3) the instructional activities that should be presented to each student. Consequently, the results of preassessment should provide information 1) as to whether any students should be required to master prerequisite skills prior to beginning instruction, 2) as to whether any students may *omit* any of the instructional objectives, and 3) for prescribing specific instructional activities for individual students.

Preassessment of Entry Behavior

Learner behaviors related to prerequisite capabilities for instruction often are called *entry behaviors*. As the term implies, entry behaviors are the behavioral capabilities resulting from previous learning that the student brings to the new instructional event. DeCecco (1974) points out that a preassessment test of entry behaviors is designed to evaluate relevant (i.e., to instructional objectives) learner capabilities resulting from previous learning. Ideally, the preassessment test of entry behaviors should be related to instructional objectives, but only insofar as the test assesses prior learning relevant to capabilities needed to master new instructional objectives.

Teachers often use various standardized tests of intelligence, achievement, and aptitude to assess students' entry behavior. These tests often are inappropriate preassessment measures, since in most instances the results cannot be used to describe students' entry behavior related to particular instructional objectives. The teacher may find some standardized personality tests and attitude tests useful in preassessing students' entry behavior regarding some affective goals; but again, these tests often do not directly relate to specific instructional objectives. Teachers are usually required to develop preassessment techniques of their own to evaluate learners' entry behavior.

Development of a preassessment test for sequentially dependent units of instruction (i.e., where mastery of each unit or course is necessary for succeeding in subsequent units or courses) can be facilitated by examining the instructional objectives employed in the preceding course(s). When previously used instructional objectives are not available or when preassessment is desired for sequentially independent units of instruction, test development may be facilitated by continuously asking and answering the question: What entering capabilities must the learner demonstrate to benefit maximally from the instruction to follow? (See Chapter 4).

While the answer(s) to this question may on the surface appear difficult to obtain, the complexity is minimized for at least two reasons. First, teachers generally are quite sensitive to the basic prerequisite skills needed for students to master given units of instruction, particularly those units taught at the beginning of a course. Second, instructional objectives provide even further guidance for the teacher in determining what prerequisite skills are needed to master given instructional units. For example, a teacher of an intermediate-level course in Spanish probably is quite sensitive to the basic capabilities that students should have mastered in a fundamental course. Moreover, by examining instructional objectives for the intermediate course (particularly those pertaining to the beginning unit[s]), the teacher should not experience extreme difficulty in answering the question: What entering capabilities must the learner demonstrate to benefit maximally from the instruction to follow? Answers to the question may result, for example, in a preassessment test designed to evaluate students' knowledge of key vocabulary words, irregular verb conjugates, and basic syntax rules. The results of the test may indicate that some or all students require additional instruction to master prerequisite skills prior to beginning instruction on the intermediate level.

Preassessment of Terminal Behavior

The second reason for preassessment prior to beginning instruction is to determine how much of what is to be learned is already known. This type of preassessment is designed to determine whether students may omit any instructional objectives. The distinction between preassessment of entry behavior and preassessment of terminal behavior is that the latter measures terminal performance (i.e., as stated in course or unit instructional objectives) prior to instruction. The clever reader will note that both types of preassessment can be accomplished simultaneously by using a test designed to assess entry behavior and terminal behavior (e.g., a portion of the test for entry and a portion for terminal). However, if for some reason the teacher must choose between the two, we recommend that preassessment focus on terminal behavior because in many instances students will have at least minimal prerequisite capabilities. Even so, a word of caution is in order. If preassessment focuses only on terminal behavior, the teacher should avoid interpreting results as indicative of entry behavior capabilities. For example, a score of zero on a preassessment test of terminal behavior does not indicate that students lack prerequisite skills; it indicates only that *they do not already know what is to be learned*. Desired information about students' entry behavior can be provided only by procedures (e.g., test items) designed to assess prerequisite skills.

When possible, preassessment test items of terminal behavior should be arranged hierarchically. This procedure is particularly useful if preassessment is to be done on a unit-by-unit basis. For example, Figure 5-1 depicts a learning hierarchy for a reading unit. One or more instructional objectives and corresponding test items may be specified for each stage of the hierarchy. Preassessment of terminal behavior would consist of test items designed to evaluate students' mastery of instructional objectives at each stage of the hierarchy. The results of this preassessment would provide the teacher with specific information about where each student is in the hierarchy and, consequently, which students may omit specific instructional objectives. For example, if the students have mastered the pronunciation of vowel and consonant sounds, then instruction would begin at stage 6.

It is important to remember that not all subject matters are amenable to hierarchical arrangement. Some subject areas are best suited to a flat structure, vertical structure, or mixed structure (see Briggs, 1968). Even so, the same basic procedure can be used for preassessment testing—e.g., assessing students' mastery of terminal behavior across the instructional objectives for a given unit and using the results to determine how much of what is to be learned students already know.

Sometimes teachers prefer to preassess students' terminal behavior across instructional objectives for an entire course rather than for one unit. This is particularly appropriate for courses in which students are allowed to "test out" of a course prior to instruction. At many colleges and universities, for example, incoming freshmen are given tests to determine

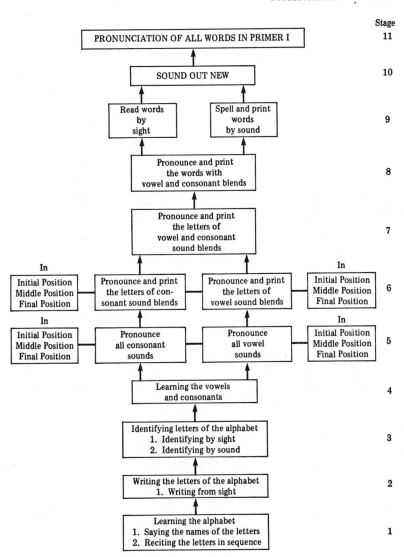

FIGURE 5-1.   Learning Hierarchy for Pronunciation of Words in Primer I

whether basic courses (e.g., math, English) are necessary. If the students indicate mastery of basic skills, then they are exempted from basic courses and permitted to take more advanced ones. When preassessment of this nature is desired, the test usually consists of items that are representative of instructional objectives within each unit of the entire course. The teacher uses the preassessment results to determine appropriate instructional placement (e.g., remedial work, advanced curriculum, etc.).

Prescribing Specific Instructional Activities

The ultimate goal of preassessment is the appropriate prescription of specific instructional activities for each student. When teachers are limited by time and/or facilities and are unable to specify individual instructional activities for students, some form of subgrouping of students is possible. This solution is, of course, most undesirable for sequential subjects such as reading and mathematics, since many students are typically "passed" to the next course or grade without having achieved the level of performance considered necessary for succeeding in the next course. These students eventually build up a cumulative deficiency that makes academic success impossible. In subjects and courses that are not sequentially dependent, it is probably unnecessary to attempt to get all students to master the same level of achievement. When this is the case, different performance standards may be specified for different individuals or groups, and this can be done on the basis of the student's preassessment performance.

Hopefully the trend toward individualized, self-paced instruction will continue and will eventually reduce or eliminate the problems inherent in instruction that is group-paced and controlled by fixed time schedules for completing units and courses. Additional strategies available to the teacher for instructing several groups of students at various levels of achievement include performance contracting and peer-group instruction. (Specific instructional activities are included in Chapter 6.)

Additional Comments About Preassessment

Preassessment is probably most important when an instructor is beginning a unit of instruction and is unfamiliar with students' skills, knowledge, and attitudes regarding the material to be covered. However, in situations where instructors have the same students for a semester, a year, or longer, preassessment for each unit may be unnecessary. In courses that are sequential in nature, the successful completion of one unit should serve as evidence of the student's ability to enter the next unit. Thus an extensive preassessment would only be necessary at the beginning of a course sequence or semester.

For shorter units (e.g., one week to a month) not in a sequential progression, less extensive preassessment would be appropriate. A few items from the end-of-unit evaluation could be used. A short interview with each student or an informal class discussion could be employed to reveal the general level of students' preparation for beginning the unit. By such informal techniques students who appear to have either considerable knowledge or inadequate knowledge regarding the objectives to be achieved for a unit can be identified and provided with a more extensive preassessment to determine what specific objectives can be omitted and what specific prerequisite skills are necessary.

An extensive discussion of the various methods of preassessment is beyond the scope of this book. It is important for the teacher to employ some method of preassessing students' entry behavior and terminal behavior to determine the most appropriate instructional procedures for achieving instructional objectives. Teachers may find the appropriate assistance in developing valid preassessment methods by examining one of the several valuable sources on test construction and evaluation (e.g., Popham and Baker, 1973; Popham, 1973; Wittrock and Wiley, 1970; Bloom, Hastings, and Madaus, 1971).

Needs Assessment

In the first part of this chapter we explained how preassessment is used to measure student ability and/or knowledge prior to instruction. Just as it is important for teachers to know their students' abilities and/or knowledge before instruction begins, it is also important for teachers to determine skills that students will need in the future. One method of identifying these skills is by conducting a needs assessment. Needs assessment helps to identify skill discrepancies and suggest actions to take based on the discrepancies. Preassessment is essentially needs assessment at the classroom level, but the important distinction between the two is that needs assessment can be conducted for individual classes, grade levels, particular schools, school districts, school regions, etc. Just as with preassessment, those using needs assessment typically ask three questions: Where are our students now? Where do we want them to be? and, How do we get them from here to there? (Sarthory, 1977).

Since the increase of state and federal laws requiring accountability for educational programs, needs assessment has become an integral part of educational planning and evaluation. Needs assessment identifies what is occurring in a particular school system and pinpoints problems in learning outcomes and processes (Witkin, 1977).

Along with the evaluation of an entire school system, it is important to evaluate goals in the classroom. Skills should be evaluated in cognitive, psychomotor, and affective domains. One method is to personalize goals in terms of objectives, activities, and evaluation. Berrie (1977) presents a set of questions in Table 5-1 to help teachers identify discrepancies between goals and current teaching procedures. These questions help to correlate goals, objectives, evaluation, and resources in the classroom.

Essential Factors

According to Berrie (1977), a needs assessment has four essential factors. A needs assessment: 1) predicts skills needed in the future, 2) identifies characteristics of local students, 3) documents activities and successes of the current educational process, and 4) determines what should be eliminated, modified, or added to the current educational process.

It is important for a needs assessment to predict future student needs. If students fail to learn basic skills, then they may be unable to master more complex skills later. For example, if students are poor in the use of addition and subtraction, then without further instruction, they will probably be unsuccessful at multiplication and division. Through needs assessment, school systems locate priority areas and provide necessary skills training.

TABLE 5-1. Questions that Can Be Used to Correlate Goals, Objectives, Evaluation, and Resources in the Classroom

Goal or Predicted Skill

	Cognitive Questions	Psychomotor Questions	Affective Questions
Classroom Objective Statements	What do I want my students to *know* because of this goal?	Is there a psychomotor skill associated with this goal?	What attitudes should students have in learning and applying this goal?
Classroom Evaluation	How can I tell the difference between successful and unsuccessful students?	How can the success of the psychomotor skills be observed?	How can I make subjective attitude evaluation less subject to individual whim and prejudice?
Methods and Materials	What processes and materials have worked in getting this goal across to the unique students in my classroom?	What processes and materials have worked in developing psychomotor skills needed for meeting this goal?	What can my students and I do together to develop the give-and-take necessary to foster attitudes needed in accomplishing this goal?
Needed Resources	What resources are needed in my classroom to better accomplish this goal?		

From P. J. Berrie, "Assessing Instructional Needs in Your District," *The Clearing House*, Vol. 50, January 1977, pp. 221–223.

Specific student characteristics must also be identified to learn about group and individual needs. A needs assessment collects information from such sources as family histories, achievement scores, future goals, and present attitudes to determine what makes these individuals or groups unique from other individuals or groups. The information, hopefully, provides data about skills the students will need to function effectively.

After student characteristics are compiled, the current educational process is analyzed. By looking at current practices and procedures, preliminary indications are made as to what should be expanded, omitted, or adjusted in the current school system. If the needs assessment indicates students are reading at their appropriate levels, then implementing a remedial reading program would probably not be necessary.

Finally, after obtaining data about necessary future skills, student characteristics, and school operations, a plan of action must be formulated. Decision makers need to identify discrepancies in the future needs and what is presently being accomplished in the school system. The discrepancies then become priority improvement areas with teachers adjusting their instructional strategies accordingly.

Systematic Process

The educational process is composed of a complexity of interacting elements. Whenever problems occur we look at teacher ability, student achievement, instructional strategies, etc., to find solutions to our problems. Often we examine causes based on hunches and/or past experience, but if we are to gain a complete understanding of the educational process we need to examine it systematically.

A systematic approach focuses on the components of the educational system that are most likely to affect the quality of learning. It is difficult for educators to see the total picture when they examine only one element in the system. With systems analysis, the basic elements are determined to help put larger goals in perspective. The ability to understand the relationships in the educational process increases our power of explanation and prediction. Just as our model of instruction is a building process, so is needs assessment.

Most needs assessment techniques follow the systematic

educational plan of Kaufman (1972). The four steps in the "classical" model of assessing educational needs are: 1) generate goals and rank them for importance, 2) determine the present status of each goal, 3) identify and analyze discrepancies between the goals and the present status, and 4) assign priorities to the discrepancies.

For example, if a group of fourth grade teachers were concerned about the results of their arithmetic program they might conduct a needs assessment to determine whether their instructional objectives were appropriate. Each teacher would submit personal instructional objectives. The objectives would be combined and the teachers would rank them in order of importance. After the objectives were ranked, teachers and students would be surveyed to see if the goals were being achieved. If certain objectives (e.g., ability to apply arithmetic to everyday situations) were not being achieved, then the teachers would identify and analyze the problem areas. Finally, the problems indicated by the analysis would become important areas of need and programs would be adjusted to meet these student needs.

As you can see, needs assessment is very similar to the steps we follow with our general model of instruction. First, we identify goals or objectives; second, we preassess to find the present status of knowledge and/or ability of the students; third, we assess discrepancies to aid in our instructional design and evaluation; and finally, we assign priorities and give feedback. The preceding example described an initial classroom need and then a common need of a group of classrooms. Needs assessment can systematically indicate the needs of a single classroom or an entire school district. Teachers, administrators, and parents might get together to suggest long-range goals and instructional objectives for their students. Through needs assessment the objectives could be evaluated to see if they are being met, in what grade level, and at what proficiency. If the objectives (goals) are not being met satisfactorily, then other instructional procedures would be used.

Model Taxonomy

At this point you may be asking: Where do I start with needs assessment? Without proper training, most teachers will require professional assistance to conduct an accurate needs assessment. However, for those of you with training, Kaufman (1977) presents possible needs assessment models and suggests a systems approach model. The broad taxonomy provides information about what does and does not constitute a needs assessment.

Models and Instruments

Many kits, models, and tools are available for implementing needs assessment programs. Everything from pre-packaged needs assessment kits to locally designed procedures can be used. According to Witkin (1977), models and instruments can be grouped into the following areas: 1) goal rating procedures, 2) methods for gathering performance and other data on existing conditions, 3) discrepancy survey questionnaires, 4) complete kits for school use, 5) futuring techniques, 6) specialized techniques, 7) regional and state models, 8) community occupational needs assessment, and 9) communication-focused methods.

Goal Rating Procedures. Goal rating is a system of ranking goals by importance and giving them priorities for program development. Common methods of goal ranking include rating by scales (Likert, etc.), card sorts, budget allocation, paired-weighting procedures, and magnitude estimation scaling. (For additional information, see Kerlinger, 1973.)

Data Gathering on Existing Conditions. Survey questionnaires are used most frequently to determine the present status of goals. (See Delphi Technique, Helmer, 1967.) Although needs assessment usually relies upon student performance data and perceptions of goal attainment, other information such as socioeconomic data, absenteeism, and racial and ethnic backgrounds can be beneficial in determining goal status. The integration of various types of data is difficult to assimilate. Two models that help minimize the difficulties are the Quality Educational Program Study of Bucks County and the Alameda County Needs Assessment Model. They are useful in selecting high priority areas.

Discrepancy Survey Questionnaires. Many publishers have developed discrepancy survey questionnaires for wide circulation. They are usually computer scored and have predetermined lists of goals and/or conditions. The tests are easily custom-tailored to suit most school systems. Some popular discrepancy survey questionnaires include Battelee's surveys (for secondary schools and colleges), Westinghouse surveys (for secondary schools), Institutional Goals Inventory (for colleges and universities), and Student Reactions to College (for community and junior colleges).

Complete Kits for School Use. Besides discrepancy questionnaires, decision makers have other kits available to them. These usually require decision makers to be more instrumental in developing parts of the procedure. Some popular kits available are the Elementary School Evaluation Kit: Needs Assessment, the Alameda County Needs Assessment Model (3rd Ed.), the Phi Delta Kappa, the Quality Education Program Study, and the Pupil-perceived Needs Assessment.

Futuring Techniques. Present planning is influenced by possible future conditions, and many school districts are interested in predicting future as well as current educational needs. A few futuristic approaches include the Atlanta Assessment Project (needs of young people in 1985), Project Redesign (societal trends), Project Simu-School (school planning), and Project SWEP (Skyline Wide Educational Plan).

Specialized Techniques. More and more school systems are specializing their needs assessment. Two popular specialized techniques to determine specific needs for the Critical Incident (CI) Method, and Fault Tree Analysis (FTA). CI was designed to identify critical factors in human performance, while FTA predicts the most probable ways a system may fail, in order to prevent failure.

Regional and State Models. Because of the stress of accountability in program planning, many regional and state assessment models have been developed. Approaches include telephone interviews, written questionnaires, public opinion polls, and conferences. A variety of survey techniques are used because of the difficulty of assessing large geographic areas.

Community Occupational Needs Assessment and Communication-focused Methods. The last two areas of needs assessment models are Community Occupational Needs Assessment and Communication-focused Methods. The Community Occupational Needs Assessment was developed to determine occupational needs of the service areas of community colleges by analyzing intergovernmental data. Communication-focused Methods emphasize in-depth communication with the public using mass media, group interviews, and other means.

From the preceding discussion, you can see that there are a variety of options available when conducting a needs assessment. However, needs assessment is still a time-consuming, expensive technique and designers have a long way to go before there will be a comprehensive, inexpensive, and expedient method of assessing a school system's needs. (Appendix D provides sources for needs assessment materials.)

Problems and Prospects

Needs assessment is a technique that identifies discrepancies between the real and the ideal in the organizational system. Needs assessment is widely accepted because it identifies discrepancies between current and desired achievement, evaluates instructional appropriateness, indicates how to change educational strategies, and suggests proper timing for changing educational goals. Even though educational administrators respond favorably to needs assessment, there are problems that reduce its effectiveness in school systems (Sarthory, 1977).

One problem in needs assessment is a lack of training. Since most administrators are familiar with the terminology, many assume that they are informed on its theory and application. Oftentimes, administrators' confidence hinders them from obtaining additional training in needs assessment application. Needs assessment implemented without necessary training often causes poor outcomes in analysis. Decision makers can receive training in implementing needs assessment strategies at the Kansas Academy for Leadership Development to alleviate this problem.

Another problem involves conceptual misunderstanding of needs assessment terminology. A *need* is "a quantifiable, measurable gap in performance, attitude, or achievement between the ideal and the real" (Sarthory, 1977, p. 24). Some people view need as a desire or as a goal. A need is not what is wanted in the future, but is the discrepancy between the ideal (what ought to be) and the real (what is). Definitions must be used uniformly in needs assessment for there to be effective outcomes.

Problems in understanding can be solved with additional training. However, a problem in organizational school structures is not solved as easily. Most school systems are small and lack adequate personnel for effective and efficient needs assessment management. Because of the complexity of the needs assessment system, some school systems generalize from one school for an entire district. Without the proper input and involvement from individual school systems, there is a likelihood of error in analysis and applicability. Many school systems are implementing needs assessment by using prepackaged kits to remedy this problem.

Externally-imposed needs can also cause problems in school systems. States often have rules, policies, and regulations that are required of all school districts. These requirements may involve special education or other procedures. Instead of locally-controlled school systems, there is state control that restricts how funds and time are to be allocated. School systems need to work cooperatively with state regulatory agencies so that local educators can provide input about particular problems and needs of each school.

Along with externally-imposed needs, local administrators begin to play "federal government games." Priorities are based on programs that will get the most federal funding rather than on appropriate programs to meet student needs. The valid use of needs assessment procedures is restricted because of many federal and state funding regulations. Funding procedures and requirements need to be reevaluated to ensure that appropriations are benefiting the greatest number of students. Justification of time and money could be explained by the number of students affected.

A final problem is the misconception that needs assessment is a total system rather than a single element of a larger system. Locating and ranking behavior gaps is just the beginning of the process. Berrie (1977) suggests three factors for closure in needs assessment: 1) implementation, 2) evaluation, and 3) beyond (recycling). Again, Berrie's factors reinforce our general model of instruction by emphasizing the use of the total model.

When a school system decides to modify existing programs, a plan needs to be established. Decision makers should suggest both immediate and long-term objectives to be met to alleviate discrepancies between the real and ideal system. Evaluation is used to determine whether the various activities have been successful. The evaluation procedures should look at the appropriateness of the objectives and the success of the methods used to reach those objectives. Suggestions from the evaluation help to make needs assessment an ongoing process. Through reassessment, continued modification in programs, and further evaluation, educational personnel will have a better idea of how to improve the process. Practitioners need to be aware of the total process for needs assessment to be used effectively.

Summary

In this chapter, the second component of the general model of instruction, preassessment and needs assessment, has been discussed. The first portion of the chapter covered preassessment. Preassessment is used to measure student performance before instruction begins. Three purposes of preassessment are: preassessment of entry behavior, preassessment of terminal behavior, and preassessment for prescribing specific instructional activities. After explaining the purposes of preassessment, procedures were given for implementing preassessment for all three purposes.

The second portion of the chapter explained needs assessment. Needs assessment identifies skill discrepancies and suggests solutions based on those discrepancies. A needs assessment typically considers skills needed in the future, characteristics of students, activities and successes of the current educational process, and what needs to be eliminated, modified, or added to the educational process. The "classical" technique of assessing needs aims to 1) generate goals and rank them; 2) determine the present status of each goal; 3) identify and analyze the discrepancies between the goals and present status; and 4) assign priorities to the discrepancies. After presenting the classical model, a model taxonomy of needs assessment was presented and explained. Next, possible kits, models, and instruments were specified for implementing needs assessment. Finally, the problems and future prospects of needs assessment were examined.

REFERENCES

Berrie, P. J. Assessing instructional needs in your district. *The Clearing House* 50, 1977, 221-223.

Bloom, B. S., Hastings, J. T., and Madaus, G. F. *Handbook on formative and summative evaluation of student learning.* New York: McGraw-Hill, 1971.

Briggs, L. J. *Sequencing of instruction in relation to competence.* Pittsburgh: American Institute for Research, 1968.

DeCecco, J. P., *The psychology of learning instruction: educational psychology*, 2nd ed. Englewood Cliffs, N.J.: Prentice-Hall, 1974.

Helmer, O. *Analysis of the future: The Delphi method.* Santa Monica, Calif.: Rand Corp., 1967.

Kaufman, R. A. *Educational system planning.* Englewood Cliffs, N.J.: Prentice-Hall, 1972.

_____. "A possible taxonomy of needs assessments. *Educational Technology* 17, 1977, 60-64.

Kerlinger, F. N. *Foundations of behavioral research*, 2nd ed. New York: Holt, Rinehart and Winston, 1973.

Popham, W. J. *Criterion-referenced instruction.* Belmont, Calif. Fearon Publishers, 1973.

Popham, W. J., and Baker, E. L. *Classroom instructional tactics.* Englewood Cliffs, N.J.: Prentice-Hall, 1973.

Sarthory, J. A. Needs assessment and the practitioner: problems and prospects. *Educational Technology* 17, 1977, 24-26.

Witkin, B. R. Needs assessment kits, models, and tools. *Educational Technology* 17, 1977, 5-17.

Wittrock, M. C., and Wiley, D. E. (Eds.). *The evaluation of instruction: issues and problems.* New York: Holt, Rinehart and Winston, 1970.

Instructional Procedures[1]

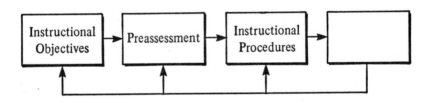

After completing this chapter, the learner should be able to:

1. Identify and explain three entry points for analyzing data from needs assessment studies;
2. State four steps involved in the design of instructional procedures;
3. Describe how each of the following is related to the design of instructional procedures:
   a) prelearning procedures
   b) learner motivation
   c) models of terminal performance
   d) active responding
   e) guidance
   f) practice
   g) knowledge of results
   h) graduated sequence
   i) individual differences
   j) classroom teaching performance

---

[1] Major portions of this chapter were adapted from David T. Miles and Roger E. Robinson, "The General Teaching Model" (Unpublished manu-

4. List and explain three organizational structures that encourage individualized instruction;
5. List ten commonly used modes of instruction and describe how each is related to the ten principles of instructional design;
6. Describe at least two ways in which research on attitudes can be applied to instruction designed to achieve goals in the affective domain;
7. List and describe five generalizations about the design of instructional procedures for achieving goals in the affective domain.

Data gathered from preassessment and needs assessment should provide instructional designers with information for developing and planning effective instructional programs. Since needs assessments are conducted using different models and instruments, instructional designers are not always certain of the types of information they will receive. Dick and Carey (1977) present three entry points to aid educators in obtaining systematically designed instruction programs that relate to specific needs identified in needs assessment studies.

At the first entry point, instructional designers would be asked to examine completed needs assessment studies. For example, home economics teachers might conduct a needs assessment to evaluate the applicability of their program. If the teachers were uncertain of how to interpret the results, they might consult an instructional designer (perhaps another teacher). When planning programs based on existing studies, designers should develop a framework for the summary and analysis of the data (i.e., task analysis), identify possible limitations in the conducted studies (such as instrumentation), and verify that the needs are unbiased, comprehensive, and valid.

At the second entry point, needs have already been documented. At this stage instructional designers must begin to identify specific instructional goals from the needs provided. Needs might include the ability to express oneself in public, the ability to pronounce unfamiliar words, or the ability to apply arithmetic to everyday situations. It is the designer's responsibility to differentiate between instructional and non-instructional needs, categorize the needs to determine the amount and type of instruction required, set priorities based on the needs with greatest impact potential, and determine

script). Educational Research Bureau, Southern Illinois University, 1969, excerpts from pp. 18–29. Reprinted by permission of the authors.

goals to identify the target group and performance conditions.

After priorities have been given to instructional needs, a program must be designed to implement instruction. (Modes of instruction are presented later in this chapter.) Designers usually follow a systematic instruction process similar to the General Model of Instruction on page 34. After writing objectives and assessing student abilities, instructional strategies and materials are developed and evaluated by members in a target population. Revisions are made in the materials and the process is repeated until the outcomes meet standards determined by the organization. In the remainder of this chapter we will examine principles to follow in designing instructional activities.

Selected Principles for Designing Instructional Procedures

The design of instructional procedures involves 1) choosing the model(s) of instruction that appears most efficient for getting most students to achieve the specified objectives; 2) selecting available instructional materials (e.g., books, films, lesson plans); 3) preparing new instructional materials when necessary; and 4) developing a sequential plan that takes students from where they are at the beginning of a unit to mastery of the unit objectives. Whenever possible, decisions about instructional procedures should be based upon sound research evidence. The ten generalizations discussed below are, to a large extent, based upon research evidence and are examples of principles that should be consulted in designing instructional activities. It should be noted that these principles will not apply to all students and all subject matters. Students vary in the way they learn, subject matters vary in their structures, and teachers vary in the way they interpret and apply principles of instruction. Thus application of these principles in each situation and with each student must be continually tested.

1. *Prelearning Preparation.* Learners must have mastered prerequisite behaviors in order to succeed in those behaviors they are required to learn. Learners also should be prepared for new learning experiences by "warming up," being informed of what previously learned behaviors will be helpful or harmful, and acquiring an appropriate "set" (predisposition to respond in a

particular way) for what is to follow. For example, a preview at the beginning of a chapter or film can increase learning efficiency. Providing students with the instructional objectives for a unit has been found to facilitate learning.

2. *Motivation.* Students are more efficient if they have a desire to learn what is being taught. This desire can be promoted by convincing learners of the value of mastering the subject matter and by making goals that they already desire (e.g., acquisition of desired information or skills, social approval, grades, etc.) available to them for accomplishing learning objectives. Selecting subject matter that interests and/or permits students to participate in planning their educational activities can also increase their desire to learn. The learning task should be presented in such a way that the learner feels challenged and also confident of ultimate success. Shaping favorable attitudes toward the subject matter, the instructor, learning, and education in general can have positive long-range consequences for student achievement.

Because motivation is such a critical variable in learning, it is treated in more depth here than the other nine instructional variables. On pp. 142 and 143 is a table entitled "Motivation for Learning." This table (6-1) is an attempt to summarize the major categories of motivation schemes. Careful study of this table will show a movement toward less abstract motivational systems from one to five. You may also feel that it is necessary to make value judgments among the five categories. Typically we place the most value on the schemes described in numbers one, two, and three, and show less preference as the motivation becomes less abstract. In all of the categories there are implications for the teacher to have some influence in motivating a student.

There is little hope in taking the position that motivation is entirely a self-generated phenomenon residing totally within the student. If one takes this position, it offers no possibilities for the teacher to shape the environment to improve motivation. In fact, whatever position one takes, it must be conceded that it is not possible to guarantee anyone's motives absolutely. Also, most people are probably operating under all of these motivation systems, depending upon the circumstances of the moment.

All of the schemes presented deal with *positive* or *non-*

TABLE 6-1. Motivation for Learning

Goal or Incentive	"The student learns (to add fractions, or write paragraphs, or build models) because . . ."	How Motivation May be Developed and Maintained
1. To know. (Delayed intrinsic)	. . . one just likes to know the how and why of things. Satisfying one's curiosity or acquiring knowledge and skill is what it's all about—whether one ever uses what is learned is unimportant (epistemic curiosity).	Provide opportunities for the student to inquire and learn about whatever is personally stimulating. Supply information and materials only when requested. Give no extrinsic rewards (praise, grades, etc.) for learning.
2. To be able to do something related to what is learned in the distant future. (Delayed intrinsic)	. . . one will eventually be able to use what is learned to do pleasureful and necessary things—i.e., read good novels, complete income tax forms, understand scientific advances, vote intelligently, raise children.	Show and frequently remind the student of the eventual value of what is to be learned. Encourage self-directed learning, minimize teacher-directed learning, and use no extrinsic rewards.
3. To be able to do something related to what is learned at the present time. (Immediate intrinsic)	. . . one needs the knowledge or skill to do something desirable now—i.e., play a game, write a poem, identify trees, communicate ideas, fix a car, train an animal, understand Apollo 11.	Provide or arrange opportunities for the student to do things that require learning. Expose potentially interesting things; pose tasks, games, questions, problems; suggest projects; supply information, materials, encouragement, and feedback; provide frequent opportunities to use what is learned.

Goal or Incentive	"The student learns (to add fractions, or write paragraphs, or build models) because . . ."	How Motivation May be Developed and Maintained
4. To obtain future benefits and rewards unrelated to what is learned. (Delayed extrinsic)	. . . one wants to pass tests, get good grades, obtain a degree, receive awards and honors, get a good job, own three cars and an Irish wolfhound; one may also want to gain the respect and admiration of parents, friends, or professional community.	Use minimal extrinsic rewards. Point out and remind the student of potential future rewards for present efforts. Use some immediate extrinsic rewards when future reward is distant, but reduce their use as student progresses.
5. To obtain immediate benefits and rewards unrelated to what is learned. (Immediate extrinsic)	. . . one wants to obtain immediate rewards such as the following: a) social rewards—smiles, verbal praise from teacher, parents, peers; b) general rewards—free time, choice of activities, money; c) specific rewards—gold star, food, toys, field trip, ball game.	Identify or develop effective rewards (reinforcers, i.e., things the student wants), systematically deliver rewards for appropriate behavior, and withhold for inappropriate behavior. Use tokens or point system to facilitate observation.

aversive styles. In each case, there is a positive or desired consequence following learning that motivates the student. There is no mention of the "other side of the motivation coin." This would be *aversive control:* motivation caused by avoidance of negative or undesirable consequences, or escape from aversive situations.

It may be that a major portion of a learner's behavior is in the form of avoidance or escape behavior. The student performs to avoid a spanking, verbal harassment, loss of privileges at home, etc. This type of motivation scheme is at times more common because it is more easily established. We often are told what bad things will happen if we do not attend class or prepare our lessons. Detention, probation, expulsion, retention in a grade, and many other things are specified as consequences for nonperformance. We have learned how to tell people what they *should not do* and the consequences involved, but we are less sophisticated in our ability to say what a student *should do* and the positive outcomes. Although the evidence from research is not conclusive, learning for desirable outcomes, as perceived by the learner, may be more effective than aversive control in achieving both cognitive and affective objectives.

3. *Providing a Model of Terminal Performance (Mastery).* Whenever possible, learners should be shown examples of what they are to produce or do at the end of a learning experience. Imitative learning is one of the most effective procedures by which human beings acquire new behaviors. For example, providing students with sample term papers, previously completed projects, final exam papers, or demonstrations of the desired performance can dramatically facilitate learning.

4. *Active Responding.* At the outset of instruction learners can profit from watching or listening to someone else perform the acts to be learned, but most learners will become proficient only if they perform the acts themselves. Thus, it is what the *learner* does—not what the teacher does—that determines learning. With verbal presentations (oral or written), interspersed questions can ensure that learners are attending to, and acquiring, what is intended. Often it is important for students to put ideas into their own words. In learning verbal material from a textbook, most students can profit by reviewing orally (e.g., reciting out loud) what they have read while not looking at the material. The stimuli to which learners attend and the

responses they make in the learning task should be matched as closely as possible to the stimuli and responses in the terminal instructional objective.

5. *Guidance.* Learners should be given guidance and prompting when attempting to demonstrate new behaviors to be learned. Such prompting should be eliminated gradually so that the learner will eventually be able to perform the task without them. For example, verbal guidance could be given at first for each step in carrying out long division problems—then the verbal prompts should be reduced gradually. Theatre directors use the guidance technique by prompting actors with their lines. As the actors learn the script verbal cues are eliminated.

6. *Practice.* Opportunities should be provided for students to use newly learned behaviors repeatedly. Since most instruction is designed to provide knowledge and skills that are to be used sometime after completing instruction, something must be done to ensure that what is learned will be retained and transferred to the postinstructional situation. *Overlearning,* which involves repeatedly using or practicing a newly learned behavior, can greatly facilitate retention. Practice and reviews spaced periodically after initial acquisition are also effective. With skills that are required to be performed in a variety of tasks and situations, practice should be provided in such variety. Practice will also be more effective to the extent that the behaviors practiced are similar to behaviors to be performed in the future (the terminal objectives). For example, after initially learning to subtract, practice with a variety of number combinations should be provided.

7. *Knowledge of Results.* Learners should have prompt and frequent knowledge of the success of their responses. The learner must find success rewarding in order for the behavior to be reinforced. Ideally, the learner should know an instant after making a response whether it is appropriate or not. Whenever possible, the learner should be provided with the criteria to evaluate the correctness of each individual response. When the learner is personally confident of the correctness of the response, external confirmation may be unnecessary, but when one is unsure, such feedback is generally desirable. When a learner's response is incorrect, information should be given as to the correct response.

8. *Graduated Sequence.* Subject matter should be organized in a hierarchical form from the simple to the complex, from the familiar to the unfamiliar. The steps should be paced so that the learner succeeds in each step but does not become bored. One approach to sequencing instruction involves a careful analysis of each terminal objective, identifying the particular stimuli to which the student responds and the responses to be made (see Briggs, 1968; Gagné, 1977). Then, by asking what the learner must be able to do (skills, knowledge) immediately prior to performing the terminal behavior, the teacher can state another objective. The same question is then asked again and again—the teacher each time specifying objectives that are prerequisite to performing objectives at the next higher stage—until eventually the instructor arrives at the behavior with which students are expected to begin the course or unit. Thus, by working backwards, a sequence of enroute or intermediate objectives are identified that should lead a student from entry to mastery of the objective. (This procedure is described in more detail in Chapter 4 and again in Chapter 7.)

It also has been found that permitting students to follow their own sequence in achieving well-defined objectives can improve upon teacher-designed learning sequences (Mager and Clark, 1963).

9. *Individual Differences.* Some students will require considerable practice to master a concept, while others may acquire the same concept upon first encounter. We already have discussed one aspect of dealing with learners' individual differences in Chapter 5, where we examined various methods of preassessment. Recall that preassessment involves the application of various testing procedures to assess learners' competencies before an instructional unit begins. As such, preassessment results can be used to tailor instructional units to suit the needs of individual students or groups of students. In Chapter 7 we discuss the concept of mastery learning, which also has relevance in planning instructional procedures that are designed to deal with individual differences in learners.

In recent years, more and more emphasis has been placed on individualized instruction. As you would assume, individualized instruction personalizes teaching strategies to meet the needs and abilities of each student. Educators view personalized instruction as a teaching alternative to meet current demands for accountability and improvement in the quality of education (Nawaz and Tanveer, 1977).

Research findings support proponents of individualized learning programs. The importance of individualized instruction is emphasized by the following general findings:

1. Children learn content at different speeds with different amounts of information retention (e.g., Dunn, 1973).
2. Students need to develop a variety of learning styles to maximize learning outcomes (e.g., Joyce, 1975).
3. Learning takes place on an individual basis (e.g., Bishop, 1971).
4. Learning requires active participation rather than just absorption of information (e.g., Stahl and Anzalone, 1970).
5. Children need to develop qualities of individuality (e.g., Heathers, 1974).

Another reason for the increased interest in individualized instruction is P.L. 94-142, or the Education for All Handicapped Children Act. Enacted on November 29, 1975, the act was designed to provide free, appropriate public education for all handicapped children between the ages of three and twenty-one. The law guarantees full educational opportunity for the handicapped. P.L. 94-142 requires educational systems to develop Individualized Education Programs (IEP) that are reviewed annually. The programs must include the child's current level of functioning, annual goals, short-term measurable objectives, and specific educational services. In addition, the act requires a comprehensive analysis of a student's learning characteristics, pre- and postassessment data, and procedures for monitoring progress.

Most current educational systems are not prepared for the far-reaching effects of P.L. 94-142. Because of the difficulty in designing programs to meet the needs of the handicapped, an upsurge of individualized planning and mainstreaming strategies has ensued. Individualized instruction appears to be a feasible solution to meet the needs of both the handicapped and nonhandicapped student. Three organizational patterns that encourage individualized instruction are: team teaching, nongraded programs, and flexible scheduling (Popham and Baker, 1973).

Team teaching characteristically includes multiple personnel with equal or differential status and responsibility.

Classes include at least one teacher, supplementary paraprofessionals, and a large group of students. With additional personnel to answer questions, students have more immediate feedback, are allowed to proceed at their own pace, and gain from divergent teacher background and experiences. *Nongraded programs* eliminate grouping students into arbitrary grade levels by age. If a twelve-year-old has the ability to master ninth grade algebra, then that child is placed in the advanced class. Each student is grouped according to individual accomplishments and abilities. *Flexible scheduling* usually includes modules of approximately twenty minutes in length. The modules are grouped together to meet individual preferences. Some units are required of all students (e.g., English, math, etc.); however, several units are left open to allow students to pursue special interests. In a history class, for example, students could independently study the Nazi Youth Movement, the reconstruction period after the United States Civil War, or causes of the Jonestown Massacre.

Many educators are hesitant to implement individualized instruction programs because they seem to require reorganization of school operations. Accordingly, schools that do not have flexible organizational structures are seeking alternative individualized instruction procedures. Without hiring additional personnel, school systems can implement team teaching by using the skills of advanced students. Those students who have mastered particular units of instruction could help students who have not, thus giving teachers more time to work with other students or to plan instructional activities. For example, if a fifth grade student successfully recites the Gettysburg Address, then that person could work with and prompt other students who have been unsuccessful.

Teachers who are interested in meeting specific student needs could incorporate nongraded units into their classrooms by combining several classes for one or two days per week. Students would be grouped according to their abilities and interests rather than by their ages. For example, English literature classes could entail reading assignments to meet the needs of groups who are college-bound, remedial, etc.

Even with a fixed time period, teachers can still employ flexible scheduling. A fifty- or sixty-minute time block can be arranged in two or three modules. For example, in a physical education class, the teacher might plan group exercises for twenty minutes and then let students pursue special interests (e.g., gymnastics, volleyball, track) for the rest of class time. These and other options are available to help meet the needs of individual students.

There is no universal model for maximum effectiveness of individualized instruction. Success of the program is dependent upon the professional and personal qualities of the teacher. Each teacher, when implementing individualized instruction, assumes such roles as consultant, manager, diagnostician, and facilitator (Nawaz and Tanveer, 1977). An individualized instruction program *does not just happen*; it must be planned. The process needs to be systematic, gradual, and evolutionary. Nawaz and Tanveer (1977) suggest the following process for implementing individualized instruction:

1. Establish instructional objectives.
2. Determine performance criteria.
3. Suggest learning alternatives.
4. Design evaluative measures.
5. Devise a system to measure the progress of each learner.

Packaged programs are also available to aid teachers in the use of individualized instruction. Three popular ones include the Individual Prescribed Test (IPT), the Computer Assisted Instructor (CAI), and the Progress for Learning in Accordance with Needs (PLAN).

It is important to remember that individualized instruction is not a panacea for all educational problems. Evaluation of instructional strategies is essential for maximum effectiveness. The system is only as good as the results it produces with each learner.

10. *Classroom Teaching Performance.* Skills in stimulating interest, explaining, guiding, identifying and administering reinforcers, and managing classroom behavior can make an enormous difference in instructional effectiveness. Unfortunately, such social skills are often the most difficult to learn, but some current work on the analysis of social and personality factors in teaching shows promise of reducing some of the complexity. The changing role of the teacher from information-dispenser to manager of instructional experiences is also an encouraging development.

Some Key Principles of Instruction

There are several distinguishable modes of instruction. The following are among the most frequently used:

1. The lecture
2. The discussion class
3. The recitation class
4. The laboratory class
5. The tutoring session
6. The demonstration
7. Independent study
8. Programmed instruction
9. Reading (books, articles, etc.)
10. Motion pictures, television, filmstrips

Each of these modes can be analyzed in terms of the extent to which each of the ten principles of instruction, described previously, can be effectively applied. The result of such an analysis can then be consulted in determining which mode or combination of modes would offer the most efficient instructional procedure for achieving particular objectives. Generally speaking,

1. Prelearning preparation can be accomplished with all modes.
2. Most modes can be employed to motivate students; however, extensive use of lectures, recitation classes, and some programmed instruction materials often has detrimental effects on student motivation.
3. Most modes can be used to provide a model of terminal performance—but, unfortunately, they are rarely used for this purpose. Demonstration is probably the most frequently used technique for showing students what they are to learn.
4. Active responding, guidance and prompting, practice, and knowledge of results are rarely provided in lectures, demonstrations, and films but are usually well provided for in tutorial and programmed instruction.
5. Most modes can be used in a progressive sequence of instruction, but again tutorial and programmed instruction are often the most systematically sequenced modes of instruction.
6. Tutorial instruction, programmed instruction, independent study, and often laboratory or studio instruction are the modes that are generally most responsive to individual differences.
7. The modes typically employed in group-paced instruction, i.e., lecture, discussion, recitation, and demonstration, usually require considerable

extemporaneous ability and a high degree of social awareness. Success with more individualized modes, i.e., programmed instruction and independent study, is more dependent upon a teacher's ability to select, prescribe, and evaluate the effectiveness of learning activities.

In selected modes of instruction, the instructor should take into consideration his/her own strengths and weaknesses. For example, if an instructor is a highly stimulating speaker, it would be reasonable to give an introductory lecture to stimulate the students' interest (motivation) in a new unit. On the other hand, an uninspiring speaker should probably use another means to motivate students—such as a film, a thought-provoking article, a field trip, a group discussion, or even a visiting speaker. Similarly, a teacher who has a tendency to dominate group discussons should either employ discussion procedures that exclude teacher participation or avoid using discussions.

While the above principles apply to instruction in all behavioral domains, we have included a special section that deals primarily with suggested instructional procedures for the affective domain.

Special Consideration of Instructional Procedures for the Affective Domain

While specific affective goals are as varied as goals pertaining to other behavior domains, instruction in the affective domain typically focuses on the establishment and/or maintenance of desirable attitudes in learners. The teacher often is concerned with establishing and/or maintaining favorable learner attitudes about the subject matter or, in some instances (e.g., social studies, sociology, and ethics), culturally-determined acceptable patterns of behavior. Consequently, the teacher may find the extensive literature on the nature of attitude and attitude change useful when devising instructional procedures to achieve affective goals. The quantity and variety of literature on attitudes precludes a thorough examination of ways it can be applied to instruction in the affective domain. However, the teacher may find the following suggestions useful and should be encouraged to develop additional instructional procedures based on principles found in the literature on attitudes.

Role Playing. Several studies (e.g., Janis and King, 1954; King and Janis, 1956; Culbertson, 1957; Scott, 1957, 1959; Janis and Mann, 1965; Wallace, 1966; Hobbs, 1975; Richey, 1975; Clark and Delia, 1976) have suggested that role playing can be an effective technique for inducing attitude change. While teachers of creative dramatics have employed role playing and improvisation techniques for years, there appears to be potentially a much wider application of these techniques for classroom instruction. For example, there is some evidence to suggest that role playing in psychodrama can be used to modify prejudiced attitudes toward minority groups (Culbertson, 1957). Other studies provide evidence that role-playing techniques can be used to modify attitudes about alcohol (Harvey and Beverly, 1961), capital punishment (Wallace, 1966), interpersonal conflicts (Bohart, 1977), and selfishness (Hull and Reuter, 1977).

Overall, the results of considerable research on attitudes suggest that various role-playing techniques can be applied to instruction in the affective domain. Moreover, role-playing techniques appear consistent with several of the previously discussed general principles related to more traditional instructional procedures, among them, motivation, active responding, and practice.

Source Credibility. Considerable research on attitudes has indicated that, in general, highly credible sources produce greater attitude change than sources low in credibility (Hovland, Janis, and Kelley, 1953; McGuire, 1969; McCroskey, 1971; Bock and Saine, 1975). While it is reasonable to assume that the teacher is considered a credible source by most learners, there appear to be additional ways in which a teacher may employ the research findings on source credibility to achieve affective goals. For example, young children often view messages on television as being highly credible (fortunately or unfortunately!). The teacher might take advantage of this fact by employing videotapes of various popular television shows that illustrate desired affective goals. In addition, the examples provided by the videotaped messages could serve as a basis for subsequent discussion and interaction with learners about relevant affective goals. A similar, but less expensive, instructional procedure might involve the use of popular recorded music to illustrate affective goals. Popular recording artists and their music play a significant part in most young people's lives. Consequently, music dealing with such socially relevant topics as ecology, race relations, and patriotism would appear an effective means for stimulating learners about relevant affective goals.

Other Suggestions. While a variety of research findings on attitudes may guide the teacher in developing instructional procedures for the affective domain, we are not claiming that these findings constitute a panacea for all of the difficulties involved with instruction related to affective goals. Moreover, we recognize that relative to other domains little attention has been given to the affective domain in terms of providing teachers with guidelines for specifying performance goals and instructional procedures. Perhaps among the few generalizations that can be made for the instructor are to 1) permit students to have as much control over what and how they learn as is feasible; 2) try to select objectives and learning experiences that would be of interest to the students; 3) provide learning activities that are challenging but with which a student can succeed; 4) attempt to win the respect and affection of your students; and 5) make the instructional environment as pleasant and comfortable as possible (from the student's point of view)—this would include concern for such obvious factors as temperature control, elimination of visual and auditory distractions, and use of comfortable furniture. In addition, the use of stimuli that have positive associations for the students might be introduced (e.g., inclusion of humor in instructional presentations, use of current and "relevant" examples to support a point, use of graphic and visual media in the contemporary idiom).

Summary

In the first part of the chapter we discussed how to use needs assessment data. Then we presented ten principles for designing instructional procedures. These principles focused on topics such as prelearning preparation, motivation, active responding, practice, knowledge of results, and individual differences. In the last part of the chapter several modes of instruction were discussed briefly, including some instructional procedures for achieving objectives in the affective domain.

REFERENCES

Bishop, L. K. *Individualizing educational systems.* New York: Harper and Row, 1971.

Bock, D. G., and Saine, T. J. The impact of source credibility, attitude valence, and task sensitization on trait errors in speech evaluation. *Speech Monographs* 42, 1975, 235.

Bohart, A. C. Role playing and interpersonal conflict reduction. *Journal of Counseling Psychology* 24, 1977, 15-24.

Briggs, L. J. Sequencing of instruction in relation to hierarchies of competence. Pittsburgh: American Institutes for Research, 1968.

Clark, R. A., and Delia, J. G. Development of functional persuasive skills in childhood and early adolescence. *Child Development* 47, 1976, 1008-1014.

Culbertson, F. Modification of an emotionally held attitude through roleplaying. *Journal of Abnormal and Social Psychology* 54, 1957, 230-233.

Dick, W., and Carey, L. M. Needs assessment and instructional design. *Educational Technology* 17, 1977, 53-59.

_____. *The systematic design of instruction.* Chicago: Scott Foresman, 1978.

Dunn, R. S. Individualizing instruction: the rationale and five alternative methods. *The Delta Kappa Gamma Bulletin* 60, 1973, 9-16.

Gagné, R. F. *The conditions of learning,* 3rd ed. New York: Holt, Rinehart and Winston, 1977.

Harvey, O., and Beverly, G. Some personality correlates of concept change through role playing. *Journal of Abnormal and Social Psychology* 63, 1961, 125-130.

Heathers, G. Education to meet psychological requirements for living in the future. *Journal of Teacher Education* 25, 1974, 108-112.

Hobbs, G. Influence of counterattitudinal acting on the attitudes of actors. *Speech Teacher* 24, 1975, 328-334.

Hovland, C., Janis, I., and Kelley, H. *Communication and persuasion.* New Haven: Yale University Press, 1953.

Hull, D., and Reuter, J. Development of charitable behavior in elementary school children. *Journal of Genetic Psychology* 131, 1977, 147-153.

Janis, I., and King, B. The influence of role-playing on opinion change. *Journal of Abnormal and Social Psychology* 49, 1954, 211-218.

Janis, I., and Mann, L. Effectiveness of emotional role-playing in modifying smoking habits and attitudes. *Journal of Experimental Research in Personality* 1, 1965, 84-90.

Joyce, B. R. Learning strategies for learning centers. *Educational Leadership* 32, 1975, 388-391.

King, B., and Janis, I. Comparison of the effectiveness of improvised versus nonimprovised role-playing in producing opinion change. *Human Relations* 9, 1956, 177-186.

Mager, R. F., and Clark, C. Explorations in student-controlled instruction. *Psychological Reports* 13, 1963, 71-76.

McCroskey, J. C. Ethos, credibility and communication in the real world. *North Carolina Journal of Speech* 4, 1971, 24-31.

McGuire, W. J. The nature of attitudes and attitude change. In G. Lindsay & E. Aronson (Eds.), *The handbook of social psychology*, Vol. III, 2nd ed. Reading, Mass.: Addison-Wesley, 1969.

Miles, D. T., and Robinson, R. E. The general teaching model. Unpublished manuscript, Educational Research Bureau, Southern Illinois University, 1969.

Nawaz, M., and Tanveer, S. A. Individualized instruction: the promise, requisites and alternatives. *Educational Technology* 17, 1977, 22-25.

Popham, W. J., and Baker, E. L. *Classroom instructional tactics.* Englewood Cliffs, N.J.: Prentice-Hall, 1973.

Richey, H. W. Role playing and modification of student attitudes. *Education* 96, 1975, 24-27.

Scott, W. Attitude change through reward of verbal behavior. *Journal of Abnormal and Social Psychology* 55, 1957, 72-75.

_____. Attitude change by response reinforcement: replication and extension. *Sociometry* 22, 1959, 328-335.

Stahl, D. K., and Anzalone, P. M. *Individualized teaching in elementary schools.* New York: Parker, 1970.

Wallace, J. Role reward and dissonance reduction. *Journal of Personality and Social Psychology* 3, 1966, 305-312.

7

Evaluation

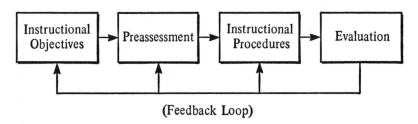

(Feedback Loop)

After completing this chapter, the learner should be able to:

1. State the primary purpose of evaluation;
2. Distinguish between a norm-referenced and criterion-referenced evaluation system;
3. Describe the steps in implementing a criterion-referenced evaluation system:
   a. State why behavior taxonomies should be used in specifying instructional objectives,
   b. Describe Gagné's method of behavioral analysis,
   c. Describe how appropriate evaluation procedures may be selected to assess students' mastery of instructional objectives,
   d. Describe what is meant by matching evaluation procedures to instructional objectives;

4. Identify and describe four selected problems in implementing a criterion-referenced evaluation system;
5. Describe the logic of a mastery-learning system;
6. Compare and contrast the mastery-learning system with the traditional system;
7. Distinguish between a mastery-learning system and a modified mastery-learning system;
8. Describe three alternative procedures that may be used to translate student performance within a modified mastery-learning system to a system requiring student performance to be expressed in terms of graduated grades;
9. Describe a grading procedure within a modified mastery-learning system that is an alternative to one that relies on a cumulative point system or average grade system.

As suggested by the feedback loop in the general model of instruction, the primary purpose of evaluation is to assess the effectiveness of instruction and to determine whether students have achieved mastery of the instructional objectives. The evaluation procedures suggested by the general model of instruction are in some ways quite different from procedures of evaluation suggested in more traditional models of instruction. Consequently, we have devoted more space to a discussion of evaluation than to other components of the model with the possible exception of instructional objectives. In this chapter we will examine the differences between norm-referenced evaluation and criterion-referenced evaluation and the procedures for implementing a criterion-referenced evaluation system. We also will examine the concept of mastery learning and how it can be applied to evaluation and grading procedures in a modified mastery-learning system.

Norm-referenced Vs. Criterion-referenced Evaluation

Current discussions about evaluation among educators often involve a comparison of norm-referenced and criterion-referenced evaluation procedures. Teachers are more familiar with norm-referenced evaluation procedures, designed to determine a student's performance *in relation to the performance of other students on the same test.* This type of evaluation procedure is referred to as "norm-referenced" because an individual's performance is compared with that of a normative group (Popham and Husek, 1969). Critical to the norm-referenced procedure is the concept of *relative standard*—i.e., the standard performance is relative to how other individuals performed on the test. For example, a relative standard might indicate that a student correctly punctuated more sentences than other students, but it does not indicate whether the student punctuated all of the test sentences, 80 percent of them, or 20 percent of them.

Criterion-referenced evaluation procedures are designed to determine whether a student has achieved mastery of a behavior *as specified in an instructional objective(s).* Both norm-referenced and criterion-referenced procedures sort students on the basis of performance, but there is an essential difference. In criterion-referenced evaluation procedures the interpretation of a student's performance is in no way dependent upon the performance of other students. Moreover, the criterion-referenced procedure assumes that if performance goals (i.e., instructional objectives) are important, teachers should be concerned with whether the student has achieved them, not with how much the student achieved relative to his/her peers (Airasian and Madaus, 1972).

The concept of criterion-referenced evaluation is not entirely new to educators. Thorndike (1918) made reference to the basic distinction between the two types of evaluation procedures, but he did not use the terms *norm-referenced* and *criterion-referenced* in his distinction. Glaser (1963) provided the initial conceptual clarity and practical implications of the two evaluation procedures that have stimulated numerous articles and papers elaborating on the applications, advantages, and liabilities of the two approaches. Table 7-1 provides a summary of the various statements that have been made comparing norm-referenced and criterion-referenced evaluation systems.

Two additional distinctions between norm-referenced and criterion-referenced evaluation procedures are noteworthy. These distinctions are related to *when* tests are given and *how* test results are used (Airasian and Madaus, 1972). In a norm-referenced system tests usually are given to students at the end of an instructional unit for grading purposes. In a criterion-referenced system tests ideally are used for at least four different types of testing purposes. First, criterion-referenced tests

TABLE 7-1. Comparison of General Characteristics of
Norm-referenced and Criterion-referenced Evaluation Systems

Norm-referenced System	*Criterion-referenced System*
1. The main function of norm-referenced evaluation is to ascertain the student's relative position within a normative group.	1. The main function of criterion-referenced evaluation is to assess whether the student has mastered a specific criterion or performance standard.
2. Either general conceptual outcomes (usually done) or precise objectives may be specified when constructing norm-referenced evaluation.	2. Complete instructional objectives are specified in the construction of criterion-referenced evaluation.
3. The criterion for mastery is not usually specified when using norm-referenced evaluation.	3. The criterion for mastery must be stated (i.e., instructional objectives) for use in criterion-referenced evaluation.
4. Test items for norm-referenced evaluation are constructed to discriminate among students.	4. Test items for criterion-referenced evaluation are constructed to measure a predetermined level of proficiency.
5. Variability of scores is desirable as an aid to meaningful interpretation.	5. Variability is irrelevant; it is not a necessary condition for a satisfactory criterion-referenced evaluation.
6. The test results from norm-referenced evaluation are amenable to transposition to the traditional grading system (A, B, C, D, F).	6. The test results from criterion-referenced evaluation suggest the use of a binary system (i.e., satisfactory-unsatisfactory; pass-fail). However, criterion-referenced evaluation test results can be transposed into the traditional grading system by following a set of specifically constructed rules.

From Mary-Jeanette Smythe, Robert J. Kibler, and Patricia W. Hutchings, "A Comparison of Norm-Referenced and Criterion-Referenced Measurement with Implications for Communication Instruction," *The Speech Teacher* 22, 1973, 4. Reprinted by permission of the authors and the Speech Communication Association.

may be used for preassessment and needs assessment purposes (see Chapter 5). Second, criterion-referenced tests may be used for formative testing (Bloom, Hastings, and Madaus, 1971)— that is, testing that is used concurrently with instruction for the purposes of checking the progress of students so that assistance may be provided when necessary. Third, criterion-referenced tests may be used to determine whether components of the instructional model (e.g., instructional objectives, instructional procedures) need modification. Fourth, criterion-referenced tests may be used at the end of an instructional unit to determine whether students have achieved the criterion levels of objectives.

Implementing a Criterion-referenced Evaluation System

The first step in implementing a criterion-referenced evaluation system is to prepare, prior to instruction, a set of instructional objectives. Most teachers will find that one or more of the taxonomies discussed in Chapter 4 will provide valuable assistance in determining what specific types of performance goals should be specified to describe the skills and competencies necessary for mastery of a particular unit of instruction. We recommend that a taxonomy (or taxonomies) be used for this purpose to avoid overemphasis of performance goals that correspond to the lower-level skills (e.g., knowledge, awareness, perception), for which instructional objectives often are most easily written. Reference to various behavioral taxonomies when developing your instructional objectives will provide guidelines to ensure that they are prepared for any necessary higher-level skills and competencies (e.g., synthesis, valuing, complex overt responses) required for mastery of the instructional unit.

The teacher may also find Gagné's (1977) task analysis (also called behavioral analysis) technique useful in preparing objectives for instructional units that primarily focus on complex cognitive or psychomotor skills (see Chapter 4). Gagné maintains that mastery of subordinate skills is necessary before mastery of superordinate skills can be achieved. Certainly this idea is not new—all teachers know that one must master basics before more advanced tasks can be mastered. However, Gagné does provide a unique and useful method for determining what are the necessary prerequisite skills for a given terminal objective. The method, called *task analysis*, is accomplished by beginning with the terminal objective for a unit of instruction (e.g., the student will be able to solve simultaneous equations) and working "downward" to the necessary behaviors for the unit of instruction. This can be accomplished successfully by asking: What must a student already know how to do in order to learn this skill? The answers to this and further questions form the set of prerequisite skills, each of which is necessary for mastery of the terminal objective. The results of task analysis often are arranged hierarchically, with the terminal objective placed at the top position, the necessary entry behaviors at the bottommost position, and the succeeding subordinate skills at various levels in between. For example, Figure 7-1[1] is a tentative learning hierarchy for an instructional unit on organizing a speech. Finally, one or more instructional objectives are then prepared for each skill specified in the learning hierarchy.

Clearly, the task analysis method ensures that instructional objectives will be specified for each type of skill or competency necessary for mastery of an instructional unit. However, the method is most applicable to units of instruction containing subject matter that can be sequenced in a hierarchical fashion and that focuses on complex cognitive or psychomotor skills. It is important to remember that development of a valid learning hierarchy for most subject areas is not an easy task. It often requires considerable time and revisions, but the benefits gained from such an analysis are commensurate with the effort it requires. Those persons who are interested in developing learning hierarchies should collaborate with others who are teaching the same content. Several persons working on the same hierarchy will save time and effort and probably will result in a more valid hierarchy.

After objectives are prepared for the unit of instruction, *the second step in implementing a criterion-referenced evaluation*

---

[1]Figure 7-1 is from Judy L. Haynes, "Improving Instruction in Speech-Communication Skills Through Learning Hierarchies: An Application to Organization," *The Speech Teacher* 22, 1973, 241. Reprinted by permission of the author and the Speech Communication Association.

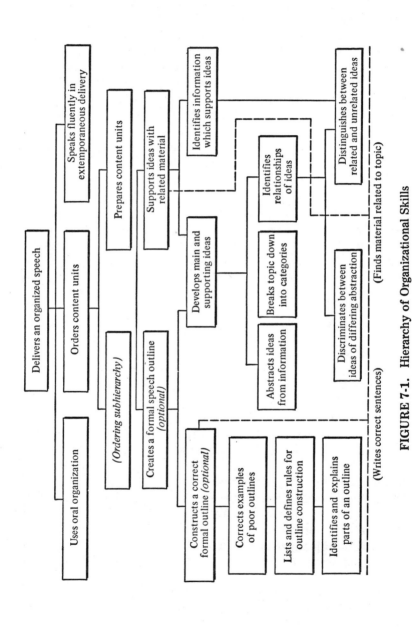

FIGURE 7-1. Hierarchy of Organizational Skills

system is the selection of appropriate evaluation procedures to assess students' mastery of stated objectives. While some form of paper-and-pencil test is used most often by teachers to assess students' mastery of instructional goals, it is not the only method of evaluation. The appropriateness of the evaluation procedure(s) selected will largely be determined by the nature of the skill or competency specified in instructional objectives. For example, consider the following instructional objectives:

1. Given twenty equations in negative integers with a missing factor, the student will apply the distributive rule in correctly supplying the missing addend in at least eighteen of the twenty equations.
2. Given twenty sentences that contain no capitalization, the student will rewrite at least eighteen sentences correctly, using the appropriate capitalization.
3. Given no books, notes, or other reference materials, the student will engage in a five-minute conversation in French with the teacher about one of the following topics: a hobby of mine, my family, last summer's vacation. Performance will be evaluated on the extent to which the student pronounces the words correctly, forms grammatical sentences, and expresses thoughts clearly.
4. Given complete freedom to select a topic of investigation of personal choice, the student will design, execute, and write a report of an experiment that meets the following criteria: there must be at least one testable hypothesis, the design must contain at least two factors of internal validity and one factor of external validity, and the results must be analyzed using at least one statistical test.

Mastery of the first two objectives would appear to be most easily assessed by some form of a paper-and-pencil test that the student would be required to take during a specified period of time in the classroom. The third objective clearly suggests that an oral-type testing procedure is most appropriate for assessing the critical skills specified in the objective, while the fourth objective suggests that a term paper might serve as an appropriate mode of evaluation. Of course, each of these objectives could be rewritten to suggest a different type of evaluation procedure, depending upon the level or type of skill/competence the teacher desires students to demonstrate. It should be clear that the teacher has considerable flexibility in selecting an evaluation procedure appropriate for assessing the particular level and type of performance indicated in instructional objectives. (For additional information concerning evaluation of criterion-referenced tests and test manuals, consult Hambleton and Eignor, 1978.)

The third step in implementing a criterion-referenced evaluation system is to match the particular evaluation procedure selected with the performance behaviors delineated in instructional objectives. It is important that the evaluation procedure(s) correspond to the level and type of behavior(s) specified in instructional objectives. If they don't, the objectives may be misleading and of little use to students, and/or the evaluation procedure(s) will not clearly indicate whether students have mastered the instructional objectives. Of course, either of these conditions is undesirable from both a teacher's and a student's standpoint. For example, consider the following instructional objectives and test items:

Objective: Given a diagram of a plant cell, the student will label in writing each of the five major components of the cell.

Test Item: Below is a diagram of a plant cell. Describe how each component of the plant cell contributes to the life of the plant and how each component interacts with other components in the cell.

Are the instructional objective and test item matched? Clearly not. The objective indicates that students should be able to identify the major components of a plant cell by labeling each component. The test item requires students to demonstrate a much higher (more sophisticated) level of behavior—i.e., describe the interrelationship and function of each component. Consequently, the objective does not clearly indicate to students the level of performance they will be expected to demonstrate. Moreover, while the test item may assess students' ability to identify and label the components of a plant cell, it is likely that the majority of students would not perform well on the test item if they only mastered the level of competency indicated in the objective. The teacher has at least two options available for correcting mismatching of this nature. The teacher can either rewrite the test item to match the objective or rewrite the objective to match the test item. For example:

Objective: Given a diagram of a plant cell, the student will label in writing each of the five major components of the cell.

Test Item: Below is a diagram of a plant cell. Label each of the five major components of the cell.

OR

Objective: Given a diagram of a plant cell, the student will label each of the five major components of the cell and describe in writing how each component contributes to the life of the plant and how it interrelates with other components.

Test Item: Below is a diagram of a plant cell. Label each of the five major components of the cell and describe how each component: 1) contributes to the life of the plant and 2) interrelates with each of the other components.

In the preceding mismatched example, the test item required students to demonstrate a higher level of behavior than what was indicated in the instructional objective. Mismatching also can occur in the opposite direction—i.e., the test item can assess students' competency at a lower level than is indicated in the instructional objective. For example:

Objective: Given one hour and no reference materials, the student will describe and synthesize in writing the series of major events leading and contributing to the United States' involvement in World War I. The product should reflect the relevant material presented in the textbook and class discussion.

Test Item: List the major events that led and contributed to the United States' involvement in World War I.

In the above example the test item requires students only to list the major events, which is a considerably lower-level behavior than indicated in the instructional objective. The objective indicates that students should be able to describe and synthesize the major events—e.g., write a well-organized essay. Mismatching of this type also is undesirable, particularly from the teacher's standpoint. Clearly, the above test item does not assess students' mastery of the instructional objective. In this particular example most students probably would perform well on the test item, but their performance would not indicate the degree to which they were able to synthesize, integrate, and clearly express ideas relating to the major events that led to the United States' involvement in World War I. Consequently, it would be possible for students to perform well on the test item without having mastered the level of skill/competency indicated in the instructional objective. Of course, mismatching of this nature may also be corrected by either rewriting the instructional objective or rewriting the test item. The two types of mismatching discussed can be avoided if teachers use a behavior taxonomy in preparing instructional objectives and corresponding test items (see Chapter 4).

To this point we have discussed and illustrated only one type of evaluation procedure—i.e., in-class paper-and-pencil test items. As indicated earlier in the chapter, instructional objectives are amenable to a wide variety of evaluation procedures. The general rule of matching evaluation procedures with instructional objectives applies to whatever specific evaluation procedure is used to assess students' mastery of stated objectives. Below are examples of instructional objectives matched to various types of evaluation procedures for different levels of behavior across the three behavioral domains.

COGNITIVE DOMAIN

1. Comprehension

Objective: Given ten questions presented orally in Russian, the student will orally answer each question in English. Performance will be evaluated on completeness of the English responses.

Evaluation Procedure: The objective suggests that an oral testing situation is most appropriate for assessment of student performance concerning this objective. The testing procedure may involve a direct one-to-one interaction between student and teacher, peer evaluations, or if the appropriate equipment is available, tape recordings may be used.

2. Analysis

Objective: Given a description of a person's attitudes about a person, object, or event, the student will select from a list of four alternatives the attitude function that is most accurately illustrated by the person's attitude.

Evaluation Procedure: The wording of this particular objective suggests that it can be matched to a multiple-choice test item. An illustrative test item might be:

Read the following passage and select the attitude function below that is *most accurately* illustrated in the event:

Tom has an inferiority complex resulting from his father's constantly harassing him about the need to "pick himself up by the bootstraps" and make a name for himself. Unfortunately for Tom, he is not very successful as an adult in term of status, occupation, and socioeconomic position. Tom is very bitter and has developed very negative attitudes about underprivileged people that have served to help him view himself as superior.

A. Adjustment Function
B. Ego-Defensive Function
C. Value-Expressive Function
D. Knowledge Function

3. Evaluation

Objective: Given one week, the student will select an experimental study reported in a journal personally chosen and write a five-page paper in which the theoretical and methodological worth of the study are evaluated. The product will be evaluated on the extent to which it reflects the criteria for evaluation of experimental research supplied to the student.

Evaluation Procedure: The objective suggests that a term paper or unit paper would be an appropriate mode of evaluation to assess students' mastery of this objective. For complicated objectives of this nature it is often helpful if students are provided with the specific criteria that will be used to evaluate their responses. For example:

The following list of criteria will be used to assess your evaluation of the experimental study you select. In your response you should provide a discussion of the worth of the study selected with respect to the following items (you may include additional items if you wish):

A. Theoretical Worth
   1. To what extent was the problem researched a significant problem for investigation?
   2. To what extent did the researcher relate the specific problem of investigation to a theoretical basis?
   3. To what extent did the research contribute to the development or expansion of knowledge?
B. Methodological Worth
   1. To what extent were the operational definitions of the independent and dependent variables specified clearly?
   2. To what extent did the experimental design reflect the principles of internal and external validity?
   3. To what extent were appropriate statistical analyses applied to the data?

AFFECTIVE DOMAIN

1. Awareness

Objective: Given two weeks, the student will prepare a written "Journal of Interpersonal Communication," containing a description of the ways in which he/she increased sensitivity to others' problems and needs in at least five different types of communication situations.

Evaluation Procedure: The product to be evaluated is clear—i.e., the written "Journal of Interpersonal Communication." However, as with many objectives in the affective domain, the criteria for evaluation are not clearly specified. Specification of rigorous performance criteria for objectives of this nature often is not desirable because they place emphasis on the indicator(s) of goal achievement rather than on the goal itself (Wright and Doxsey, 1972). Even so, the evaluation procedure suggested here could provide the teacher with some index of student growth and development in terms of interpersonal sensitivity, particularly if students were requested to prepare two "Journals of Interpersonal Communication"—one at the beginning of the term and one at the end. The teacher might then compare the two journals for each student on the basis of several possible criteria. For example, an increased sensitivity to others' problems and needs might be reflected in the nature of the communication events reported—e.g., from events involving communication with only close friends and relatives to events involving communication with mere acquaintances. Student learning might also be indexed by appropriate changes in the students' criteria for determining what is a communicative event that provides one with the opportunity to be sensitive to the needs and problems of others.

2. Valuing

Objective: Given one week, the student will observe several national and local news programs and write a five-page (minimum) paper in which the student's personal criteria are used to evaluate the worth of freedom (i.e., not censoring) in news reporting.

Evaluation Procedure: The evaluation procedure suggested in the objective is again in a written form. However, the objective could be modified to allow assessment of the student's ability to present personal thoughts orally to classmates. The oral presentation could have an additional advantage in that it may generate discussion/disagreement among students and provide an index of students' ability to tolerate differing points of view.

3. Organization

Objective: Given an art object of personal choice, the student will identify the characteristics of the object he/she admires and construct a work of art that reflects these characteristics.

Evaluation Procedure: The mode of evaluation is clear (i.e., construction of an art object) and in this case differs from the oral or written modes. While flexibility and freedom for creativity would appear important in this objective, the evaluation procedure perhaps could be made more useful if students were required to specify the characteristics that the art object they construct is supposed to reflect. The teacher and classmates might then be in a position to provide useful feedback to the student regarding the extent to which the characteristics are clearly reflected in the art object.

PSYCHOMOTOR DOMAIN

1. Set

Objective: Given no prompting or reference materials, the student will demonstrate five basic positions with a minimum rating of five by two of three judges (on a seven-point scale).

Evaluation Procedure: The use of rating scales for evaluation purposes requires the teacher to state clearly and concisely the specific criteria that will be used to assess students' performance. Once criteria are specified, it is a good idea to provide students with a copy of the rating scales so they know precisely what criteria will be used to judge their performance. Rating scales also allow the opportunity to employ peer-group evaluation, which provides students with practice in making judgments about others' performance using the same criteria that they are required to meet for their own performances.

2. Guided Responses

Objective: Given a demonstration on how to operate a wood lathe, the student will demonstrate the steps in operating a wood lathe following the recommended safety precautions outlined in the class handout.

Evaluation Procedure: While mastery of this objective could be assessed with a paper-and-pencil test, more complex psychomotor behaviors probably should be assessed under conditions that more closely approximate, or are exactly like, the actual behavior to be performed. Testing of this sort provides students with practice and also affords the opportunity for the teacher to supply immediate feedback.

3. Complex Overt Response

Objective: Given an unadjusted carburetor and one hour, the student will adjust the carburetor so it operates at maximum capacity.

Evaluation Procedure: The same comment applies here as in the preceding example.

While we have reduced the procedures in implementing a criterion-referenced evaluation system to only three steps, it should be clear that such implementation is seldom accomplished without some difficulties. More and more school districts are incorporating mastery learning into their systems. Another useful model is presented by Hambleton (1978), which helps educators develop and validate criterion-referenced measurement. The following sections are devoted to discussion of four of the most pervasive problems confronting the teacher using a criterion-referenced evaluation system.

Implementation of a Criterion-referenced System—Selected Problems[1]

———————— *Branching Option Four* ————————

The material contained in the next several pages is rather technical in nature. To obtain a firm understanding of the material, it is necessary for you to have a moderately sophisticated background in test construction, measurement theory, and statistics. However, we suggest that you read the material even if you have some question about your ability to understand it fully. Perhaps your instructor will clarify any question you may have. If you feel that you cannot understand the material, turn to page 177 and begin reading the section titled "Mastery Learning."

---

[1] Adapted from Mary-Jeanette Smythe, Robert J. Kibler, and Patricia W. Hutchings, "A Comparison of Norm-referenced and Criterion-referenced Measurement with Implications for Communcation Instruction," *The Speech Teacher* 22, 1973, 1-17. Reprinted by permission of the authors and the Speech Communication Assocation.

Determination of Criterion for Mastery

The conceptual model of criterion-referenced measurement rests upon the premise that this method of evaluation will provide valid evidence regarding a student's learning of relevant skills or concepts. Mastery, therefore, depends upon the establishment of an absolute performance standard against which the adequacy of each student's learning may be weighed and judged. Such a standard should specify the exact proportion of the skills tested that a student must exhibit before being said to have mastered some particular content; it should be absolute in the sense that it is set prior to evalution and serves as the sole criterion against which each student's performance is assessed. This inevitably raises the question of how the teacher selects the criterion values to be used. Although this is one question that is not yet satisfactorily resolved (Glass, 1978) and that is of sufficient complexity that it precludes discussion in this work of all the details involved in a criterion selection decision, some general observations seem to be warranted.

It may be useful to regard a criterion as a cutting score or a limiting value of a given proficiency range (Glaser and Nitko, 1971). (Further suggestions for administering cut-off scores are given by Hambleton (1978) and Zieky and Livingston (1977).) Typically, these criteria are expressed by stating percent values, e.g., 80 percent, 90 percent, or 100 percent, or numbers, e.g., seven of ten, twenty of twenty-five, as the minimum acceptable level of mastery. Stated in this way, the criterion values may be used to denote both the quantity and the quality demands of the instructional objective. What frequently occurs in practice when criteria are set is that the teacher initially makes an arbitrary decision based on personal experience and subsequently modifies the criterion value over time as a function of the relative importance of the behaviors being evaluated. For example, a third grade math teacher set the criterion for mastery at 75 percent for use of multiplication tables. At the end of the unit of instruction, he raised the mastery criterion to 85 percent because he found that the students required better proficiency to perform higher-level math problems. Performance norms from test administrations with previous samples of students may also provide a basis for decision making. In the absence of any concrete information

regarding student entry behavior, or the hierarchy of probable responses, raw intuition may be the only available guide to
an initial selection of the criterion value. Reliance upon the
intuitive powers of competent and experienced teachers working cooperatively is particularly helpful in setting standards.
Until a systematic set of rules applicable to a broad spectrum
of curricula is developed, the process of criterion selection will
require teacher insight and judgment.

Observation of existing criterion-referenced measurement
systems suggests at least two cautions with regard to criterion
selection (Kriewall, 1972). First, adherence to a rigid criterion
selection policy, without consideration of its consequences, is
a dubious practice. A number of factors, including the nature
of the tested material, frequency of testing, and test format
characteristics, probably interact with the criterion value and
affect student performance. Fixed criterion policies are viable
only when sampling plans have been analyzed for each unit to
ensure content validity of the criterion-referenced measurement and when considerable attention has been given to the
decision implications inherent in the selection of the test
length with the criterion value. Otherwise, the teacher may be
compelled to use irrelevant test items to maintain uniform test
lengths or, worse still, require students to attain a criterion that
is optimum for longer tests, but unrealistically high on shorter
tests.

Secondly, the mistaken belief that selecting a higher
criterion value will result in a better quality of learning product
should be abandoned. In almost all cases, this practice leads to
a high probability of false negatives because the permissible
margin for error is so narrow that the majority of tested students
may fail to demonstrate mastery. Even the most carefully constructed criterion-referenced measurement, or norm-referenced
measurement for that matter, is seldom a sufficiently stable or
representative instrument to warrant a very high (90 or 100 percent) criterion value. Moreover, teachers must consider the
affective, as well as the cognitive, consequences of performance
standards. Assuming that students can be compelled to achieve
consistently at the 90- or 95-percent level, are these cognitive
outcomes meaningful enough to offset the possibility that the
high performance standard makes instruction and evaluation
procedures repugnant to students? The problem here is to find

the admissible, if not optimum, solution that will maximize the positive development of learning, cognitively as well as affectively. Although further research to resolve this issue is indicated, available data suggest that setting the criterion for mastery at 85 percent may be optimal (Block and Anderson, 1975).

Variability

The theory and method associated with the study of measurement in psychology and education have been developed in relation to psychological testing. The measurement concept of *variability*, the extent to which a group of scores tends to be homogeneous with regard to the specific trait being measured, has a decided influence on the interpretation of test scores. According to Popham and Husek (1969), the variability problem is the central theoretical and operational distinction between criterion-referenced measurement and norm-referenced measurement. On a theoretical level, variability determines the meaningfulness of norm-referenced measurement scores. The student is evaluated in terms of the position of his/her score in comparison with all other scores on the same norm-referenced measurement. Generally, the more variability in the scores on norm-referenced measurement, the better the test. Variability is largely ignored in assigning meaning to criterion-referenced measurement scores. The student is evaluated with regard to how closely the score approximates an established standard of performance. Consequently, the degree of variability obtained in criterion-referenced measurement scores is not necessarily related to the quality of the test.

Operationally, variability exercises a powerful effect on both norm-referenced and criterion-referenced approaches to testing. Traditional methods of test development and assessment, based on variability, are available for norm-referenced measurement. However, the teacher who decides to implement criterion-referenced measurement must be prepared to alter certain measurement concepts as traditionally defined. During the past ten years, considerable progress has been made toward developing technology to diagnose student learning deficiencies, monitoring student progress, and evaluating school programs (Hambleton, 1978). A discussion of these concepts follows.

Item Analysis. Regardless of how painstakingly criterion-based tests are constructed, traditional methods of evaluating norm-referenced tests may be inappropriate for criterion-referenced measurement because these methods depend on variability of scores (Popham and Husek, 1969). However, implementation of criterion-referenced testing should not ignore comparative data (Popham, 1978). Criterion-referenced tests use normative data to create precise descriptions of each domain being measured (Hambleton, Swaminathan, Algina, and Coulson, 1978; Popham, 1976). Although one can argue that in practice the performance of students on criterion-referenced measurement may vary (Livingston, 1970), the possibility that scores on criterion-referenced measurement may have little or no variance does cast doubt on the relevance of the concept of reliability as defined within classical test theory. Still, efforts to ascertain the internal consistency of criterion-referenced measurement should not be abandoned prematurely.

In norm-referenced measurement, item analysis procedures are typically employed as a basis for rejecting items that do not properly discriminate among students taking the test. Since a criterion-referenced measurement is used to determine mastery or nonmastery of specified criterion behaviors rather than to differentiate individuals in a group, application of typical discrimination indices should be modified to accommodate the assumptions underlying criterion-referenced measurement. Cox and Vargas (1966) have suggested an index based on the percentage of students who passed an item on a posttest minus the percentage of those who passed the same item on a pretest. Generating hypothetical frequencies based on the median value of each subtest, Popham (1970) has used *chi-square* to estimate the pre- and postinstructional relationship of individual test items. Hsu (1971) has developed an item discrimination index derived from the difference between the proportion of students who attain the criterion score on a test and answer a test item correctly and the proportion of students who do not achieve the criterion score and yet who still answer an item correctly. An item that has a larger proportion of correct responses in the group failing to achieve the criterion, then, discriminates negatively and should be reconsidered.

Regarding the omission of criterion-referenced measurement test items that appear to discriminate poorly or negatively between mastery and nonmastery groups, two considerations seem to be in order. First, nondiscriminatory items are not necessarily inadequate items if they reflect an important aspect of the specified criterion behavior. If the item is indeed relevant to the performance objective, then the effectiveness of the intervening instruction may be at fault. Further, the item analyst should be sensitive to patterns in item discrimination. Should items measuring a certain class of behaviors be consistently poor or negative discriminators, then the specifications of the criterion must be questioned. In this sense, item analysis procedures may provide an empirical check on the validity of the construct that the criterion-referenced test was designed to measure (Jackson, 1970).

Reliability. An estimate of *test reliability*, the degree to which all items on a test are measuring the same behaviors, is no less desirable for criterion-referenced measurement than for norm-referenced measurement. Unfortunately, the troublesome issue of score variability, upon which classical reliability procedures are based, restricts the options available to the criterion-based test constructor. Compounding the problem is the absence of any alternative procedures that are data based and of demonstrated empirical validity. On the basis of a modification of classical reliability theory, Livingston (1972) has proposed a *criterion-referenced measurement reliability coefficient* that is derived by substituting the criterion score of a test for the mean test score in the formula for computing the coefficient. Although the procedure has been challenged by Harris (1972), Hsu (1971) cites some data demonstrating that the results obtained from Livingston's formula are roughly comparable to those obtained from the Kuder-Richardson 20 formula. [*Note*: The K-R 20 formula is only one of several definitions of internal consistency.]

A somewhat different approach, involving independently developed parallel forms of a criterion-based test, would estimate reliability through an index of agreement between the scores obtained on the two tests. In discussing this method, Jackson (1970) suggests categorizing scores according to some nominal classification and then computing a contingency coefficient to obtain a reliability estimate.

Assuming that a measure of reliability is achieved, are there methods to refine the criterion-referenced test so that it will be a more precise and stable instrument? In norm-referenced measurement the time-honored strategies are to delete ambiguous items, develop standard and clear instructions, and add more items of equal quality and kind. Completion of these operations will, likewise, facilitate the development of better criterion-referenced measurement. When the behaviors specified in the criterion are complex, the need for extra items to sample the domain adequately is particularly acute. Similarly, ambiguities in objectives, instructions, or test items are never desirable.

Perhaps the single most effective method of ensuring precision and accuracy in criterion-referenced measurement, though, is the careful matching of test items to performance objectives. When the behaviors are clearly delineated for student and teacher alike and a systematic testing plan is implemented, objectivity and accuracy should be among the consequences.

Mastery Learning

An additional concept relating to evaluation, which is particularly suited to a criterion-referenced system and which is consistent with the philosophy of the general model of instruction presented in this book, is the concept of *mastery learning*. Simply stated, mastery learning proposes that all, or almost all, students can master given instructional objectives at high standards of performance. While effective mastery-learning strategies have been developed only recently (Bloom, Hastings, and Madaus, 1971; Schmieder, 1974; Cappuzzello, 1976; Westbrook and Sandefur, 1975; Pittman, 1975), the concept of mastery learning is not entirely new (Washburne, 1922; Morrison, 1926). However, the recent interest in and development of effective mastery-learning strategies received impetus from Carroll's (1963) model of foreign language learning. Carroll found that students' ability to learn language predicted not only the level of competency they attained in a given time period, but also the amount of time students required to attain a given level of competency. Consequently, rather than viewing student aptitudes as an index of the level of learning that could be attained, Carroll defined aptitudes as an index of the amount of time students required to master a given criterion level under ideal instructional conditions (Block,

1971). In effect, Carroll's model proposed that if a student were allowed the time needed to master given subject matter content and if the required time were spent in appropriate instructional activities, then it could be expected that the student would attain mastery of the subject matter.

In a later article dealing with the concept of mastery learning, Bloom (1968) argued that if students were distributed normally with respect to aptitude for a given subject and if they received the same instruction (i.e., in terms of quality and time), then student achievement would also be normally distributed (Block, 1971; Block and Anderson, 1975).[2] This is illustrated in Figure 7-2. Bloom's argument in effect describes the traditional, norm-referenced type of evaluation system that characterizes most current educational systems.

Following Carroll's (1963) model, Bloom (1968) further argued that if students were distributed normally with respect to aptitude but received quality instruction and were allowed needed time to master content, then one could expect little or no relationship between aptitude and achievement, as suggested in Figure 7-3.[3]

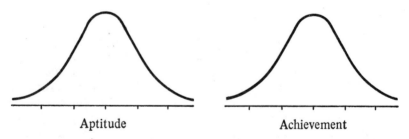

Aptitude   Achievement

FIGURE 7-2.   Aptitude and Achievement in the
Traditional Norm-Referenced System

[2] Most research on aptitude and achievement suggests only a 30- to 40-percent correspondence rather than a one-to-one correspondence. Also, it should be noted that, technically, random error is the only thing that is distributed normally, not psychological traits, as indicated in the curves in Figures 7-2 and 7-3. The curves are depicted as they are for illustrative purposes.

[3] Note that achievement in a pure mastery-learning system is more appropriately depicted as a bimodal curve indicating mastery or nonmastery of objectives. However, in a modified mastery-learning system where student

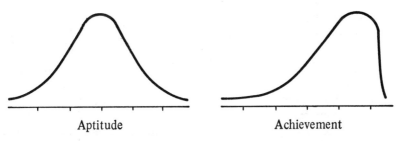

Aptitude   Achievement

FIGURE 7-3. Aptitude and Achievement in the Mastery-Learning System

The key aspect of the mastery-learning system is that it allows each student to spend whatever time is needed to master content before being presented with new material. Consequently, in the pure mastery-learning system students are allowed unlimited opportunities to demonstrate mastery of instructional objectives. As such, application of a pure mastery-learning system is obviously not practical for most current educational systems. However, there are alternatives to a pure mastery system. One alternative is what we shall refer to as a modified mastery-learning system, which is examined in the following section.

The interest in mastery learning has generated school-based research at all levels of education. Mastery learning is used effectively with student-teacher ratios of twenty or thirty to one and with seventy to one and above (Block and Anderson, 1975). Results from mastery-learning research (Block, 1974; Block and Burns, 1976) suggest that:

1. Two to three times as many students achieve the equivalent of A or B grades when learning by mastery as compared to nonmastery techniques.
2. Mastery-learning methods yield better retention and transfer of material than nonmastery approaches.
3. Mastery approaches yield greater interest and more positive attitudes in subjects learned than nonmastery approaches.

---

performance is translated into a standard grading format (i.e., A,B,C,D,F), achievement is more appropriately depicted as it is in Figure 7-3. The next section will examine grading procedures with a modified mastery-learning system.

4. Mastery methods have aided students in learning how to learn by providing variety, selectivity, and self-reward in learning experiences.

Table 7-2 (pp. 180-181) is designed to illustrate and summarize the fundamental differences between a traditional and a mastery-learning system. While some of the contrasts presented in the table may appear overgeneralized, they have been so designed to stress the extremes inherent in the two systems.

TABLE 7-2.   Contrasts of Selected Characteristic Assumptions of the Traditional Education Systems and Mastery Learning

Traditional System	Mastery-Learning System
1. Students entering a course/school year have approximately the same competencies.	1. Students have varied entering behaviors (competencies) at the beginning of instruction for a course/school year.
2. For efficiency, students are grouped into three basic learning levels, i.e., superior, average, and slow learners.	2. Students are not grouped but are assessed on an individual basis.
3. Course planning is usually oriented toward the material to be covered.	3. Course planning is oriented toward desired terminal performances.
4. The teacher's role is primarily that of an information-dispenser.	4. The teacher's role is primarily that of a learning manager, e.g., selecting and developing appropriate instructional strategies based on individual students' needs to achieve objectives.
5. A given instructional strategy is selected and designed to be most effective and efficient for most students.	5. Instructional strategies are selected and designed for individual competencies and learning styles.
6. Generally, instruction focuses on the "average" student.	6. Instruction focuses on the individual student.

TABLE 7-2. (Continued)

Traditional System	Mastery-Learning System
7. Responsibility for achievement rests primarily with the student.	7. Responsibility for student achievement is primarily the teacher's (or is shared with student).
8. Students achieve in a normally distributed manner that is reflected in their performance.	8. Students achieve at or above a given level of mastery (previously specified criterion) that is reflected in their performance.
9. A student's performance is often evaluated by comparing *it* with that of other students.	9. A student's performance is evaluated by comparing *it* with an absolute standard (pre-specified criterion).
10. Periodic assessments (e.g., midterms, unit tests, quizzes) are for determining the current levels of achievement, and the student almost always continues *regardless* of performance.	10. Formative (periodic) evaluations are for diagnostic purposes and are independent of the summative (final) evaluation, the result of which is to recycle students' learning or permit them to progress.
11. Periodic evaluations and/or final exams are used to determine a final grade, usually by some averaging procedure.	11. Summative evaluations are for grading (i.e., determining if criterion has been achieved) such as a pass-fail or S-U procedure.
12. The necessity for recycling (repeating) is determined only at the conclusion of the course/school year.	12. Recycling is necessary at any stage of the instruction at which criterion is not met.
13. Students leaving a course/school year have a wide range of competencies in achieving the general objectives.	13. Most (ideally, all) students achieve a previously established, criterion level of mastery before beginning the next segment of instruction.

From G. Robert Spell, Robert J. Kibler, and Arlie Muller Parks, "A Comparison of Mastery and Traditional Learning Systems with Selected Implications for Speech Communication Instruction." Paper presented at the meeting of the International Communication Association, Atlanta, Georgia, April 1972. Reprinted by permission of the authors.

Modified Mastery Learning

As already indicated, implementation of a pure mastery-learning system is in most instances impractical within the currently established educational systems. An alternative to a pure mastery-learning system is what we prefer to call a *modified mastery-learning system.* The modified system differs from the pure system in two ways that are important to concerns about practicality regarding implementation. The modified mastery-learning system places a limit on 1) the amount of time given to students to demonstrate mastery of instructional objectives and 2) the number of opportunities students have for demonstrating mastery of instructional objectives.

Regarding the limitation of time, students in a modified mastery-learning system are required to master instructional objectives for an entire course within the specified time limit determined by the educational system (e.g., a semester, a quarter, a year, etc.). The specific working procedures for implementing the system usually can be left to the teacher's discretion. For example, a teacher may require students to master objectives for a given unit of instruction within a specified time limit (e.g., two weeks, three weeks, etc.), or the teacher may allow students to recycle through units at their own pace as long as they complete all units of the course within a specified period of time. Decisions about specific working procedures depend upon such matters as the nature of the subject matter (e.g., sequentially dependent or independent units), the availability of individualized instructional materials (e.g., programmed texts, reading materials), student preferences, and limitations on the teacher for spending time with students who need additional instruction. Usually a teacher can find some means for implementing a workable system within the particular limitations of time and facilities of the educational institution.

The second aspect of the modified mastery-learning system can be implemented by using multiple test forms for each unit of evaluation in the course. The number of test forms employed would then serve to define the number of chances students have to improve performance on a particular unit of instruction. For example, if a course consisted of three units, a teacher might develop four forms of each unit test (e.g., a total of twelve tests). For each unit of the course, students would then be given a maximum of four chances to improve mastery of the objectives. It is difficult to offer a general statement about how many test forms a teacher should use. The decision would be determined, in part, by limitations of time and the nature of the subject matter. However, we suggest beginning with at least two forms of each test. Examining the results of student performance across a few quarters (terms, years, or whatever) would help the teacher determine if two forms of each test appear to provide enough opportunity for most students to succeed in the course at a fairly high level. If this turns out to be the case (our own experience indicates that it usually is), there is no need to develop additional test forms. However, if examination of student performance suggests that the majority of students need additional opportunities to demonstrate mastery, then developing and employing additional test forms should be considered.

Grading in a Modified Mastery-Learning System

When an educational institution employs a *dichotomous* grading system, such as pass-fail or satisfactory-unsatisfactory, as an index of student achievement, there is little or no problem in implementing a modified mastery-learning system. However, in most instances educational institutions use a *graduated index* of student achievement (e.g., A, B, C, D, F). When a graduated index is used, the teacher must be able to translate student performance within the mastery-learning system into the type of grading procedure used by the school system. A way of making this translation is to set criterion levels for minimum acceptable performance that correspond to the grading scale of the educational institution. One method for achieving the correspondence is for the teacher to require that a prespecified minimum number—or percentage—of instructional objectives be mastered for each particular grade level. For example, the teacher might require students to master 90 to 100 percent of the objectives for a given unit of instruction in order to receive an A, while mastery of 80 to 89 percent of the objectives would be required to attain a B, and so on. While this strategy can be used to translate grades from a mastery system to a traditional one, there is at least one problem in using this particular method. The method implies that all (or most) of the objectives for a given unit of instruction are of equal value in terms of complexity and/or importance. In other words, this method makes it possible for a student to obtain an A, for example, for a given unit of instruction even though failing to demonstrate mastery of some of the most important objectives for the unit. An alternative to this method is to classify the objectives for a given unit of instruction into separate categories based on their importance, value, and/or complexity. The teacher then might specify minimum criterion levels for mastery of objectives within each category. For example, students might be required to master all of the objectives in one category and only 90 percent of the objectives in another category in order to receive an A for a given unit of instruction. This method also has drawbacks, since it may require the teacher to keep complicated progress reports on each student to determined which category of objectives has been mastered and which has not. The method also might entail an exorbitant amount of paper work for the teacher during retesting with alternative forms to ensure that each student is being retested over the appropriate category or categories of objectives. A third alternative, and by far one of the easiest, is to include a representative sample (in terms of importance and/or complexity) of objectives on each test over a given unit of instruction. The sample of objectives for inclusion on the test should be such that a high level of performance cannot be attained on the test unless a reasonable number of important/complex objectives have been mastered. If this condition is met, then mastery of a minimum number or percentage of objectives for each grade level may be specified without the potential problems of the first alternative.

A final note should be made about grading in a modified mastery-learning system. The teacher should avoid using a grading procedure that relies on a cumulative point system or averaging of grades across instructional units to determine students' final grades for a course. Such procedures make it possible for students to obtain a moderate to low (e.g., B to D) level of mastery for one or more units of instruction and still obtain a high level of mastery (e.g., an A) for the entire course. While this may not appear problematic on the surface, it does in effect negate the logic of a criterion-referenced, mastery-learning evaluation system. Ideally, a grade of A in a mastery-learning system indicates that a student has mastered the objectives across all units of a course at an A level. However, since we are concerned with implementation of a modified mastery-learning system, wherein limits are set on the amount of time and test opportunities students have to demonstrate mastery, the teacher may consider such ideal standards too stringent to be implemented practically. If this is the case, the teacher may devise a set of rules for determining final course grades that allow for more flexibility (i.e., room for student error). Incidentally, it probably is a good idea to build some flexibility of this nature into the grading system to account for possible measurement error. An example of a flexible grading system might be one following rules similar to these for a four-unit course:

To obtain an A in the course, you must:

1. Obtain an A on each unit test (first *or* second form) plus an A on the outside project;

OR

2. Obtain a total of three A's on unit tests and/or the outside project and *only one B.*

To obtain a B in the course, you must:

1. Obtain at least a B on each unit test (first *or* second form) and at least a B on the outside project;

OR

2. Obtain a total of at least three B's on unit tests and/or the outside project and *only one C.*

To obtain a C in the course, you must:

1. Obtain at least a C on unit tests (first *or* second form) and at least a C on the outside project;

OR

2. Obtain a total of at least three C's on unit tests and/or the outside project and *only one D.*

To obtain a D in the course, you must:

1. Obtain at least a D on each unit test (first *or* second form) and at least a D on the outside project;

OR

2. Obtain a total of at least three D's on unit tests and/or the outside project and *only one F.*

To obtain a F in the course, you may:

1. Fail to take either form of the unit tests and/or fail to complete the outside project;

OR

2. Perform below the minimum requirement for a D on *two* or more unit tests or one unit test *and* the outside project.

Summary

This chapter has focused on the fourth component of the general model of instruction. Our discussion of evaluation procedures in the model hinged on two concepts: criterion-referenced evaluation and mastery learning. Criterion-referenced evaluation was defined and distinguished from the traditional norm-referenced evaluation system. The procedures for implementing a criterion-referenced evaluation system were outlined. These procedures included: 1) the specification of instructional objectives, 2) the selection of appropriate evaluation procedures to assess students' mastery of stated objectives, and 3) the matching of particular evaluation procedures with performance behaviors specified in objectives. The section on criterion-referenced evaluation ended with an examination of selected problems in implementing a criterion-referenced system.

The section on mastery learning described the work of Carroll (1963) and Bloom (1968) in formulating the basic logic of a mastery-learning system. It was suggested that implementation of a pure mastery-learning system is in most instances impractical. Consequently, the procedures for implementing a modified mastery-learning system were presented. The modified system differs from the pure system in two ways that are important regarding the practicality of implementing the system. The modified mastery-learning system places a limit on 1) the amount of time given to students to demonstrate mastery of instructional objectives and 2) the number of opportunities students have for demonstrating mastery of instructional objectives. The chapter concluded with an examination of various procedures for translating student performance within a modified mastery-learning system into a graduated grade index.

REFERENCES

Airasian, P. W., and Madaus, G. F. Criterion-referenced testing in the classroom. *The National Council on Measurement in Education (NCME)* 3 (4), 1972, 1-8.

Block, J. H. The effects of various levels of performance on selected cognitive, affective and time variables. Unpublished doctoral dissertation, University of Chicago, 1970.

_____. Introduction of mastery learning: theory and practice. In J. H. Block (Ed.), *Mastery learning: theory and practice.* New York: Holt, Rinehart and Winston, 1971.

_____. Standards and criteria: A response. *Journal of Educational Measurement* 15, 1978, 291-295.

Block, J. H. (Ed.) *Schools, society, and mastery learning.* New York: Holt, Rinehart and Winston, 1974.

Block, J. H., and Anderson, L. W. *Mastery learning in classroom instruction.* New York: Macmillan, 1975.

Block, J. H., and Burns, R. B. Mastery learning. In L. Shulman (Ed.), Review of Research in Education, Vol. 4. Itasca, Ill.: F. E. Peacock, 1976.

Bloom, B. S. Learning for mastery. *Evaluation Comment* 1, 1968.

Bloom, B. S., Hastings, J. T., and Madaus, G. F. *Handbook on formative and summative evaluation of student learning.* New York: McGraw-Hill, 1971.

Cappuzzello, P. G. Personal letter dated August 11, 1976, describing the work of the Academic Development Resource Center, Bowling Green State University, in annotating CBE documents.

Carroll, J. A model of school learning. *Teachers College Record* 64, 1963, 723-733.

Cox, R. C., and Vargas, J. S. A comparison of item selection techniques for norm-referenced and criterion-referenced tests. Symposium presented at the meeting of the American Educational Research Association and the National Council on Measurement in Education, Chicago, February 1966.

Gagné, R. M. *The conditions of learning*, 3rd ed. New York: Holt, Rinehart and Winston, 1977.

Glaser, R. Instructional technology and the measurement of learning outcomes: some questions. *American Psychologist* 18, 1963, 519-521.

Glaser, R., and Nitko, A. J. Measurement in learning and instruction. In R. L. Thorndike (Ed.), *Educational measurement*. Washington, D.C.: American Council on Education, 1971.

Glass, G. V. Standards and criteria. *Journal of Educational Measurement* 15, 1978, 237-261.

Hambleton, R. K. On the use of cut-off scores with criterion-referenced tests in instructional settings. *Journal of Educational Measurement* 15, 1978, 277-290.

Hambleton, R. K., and Eignor, D. R. Guidelines for evaluating criterion-referenced tests and test manuals. *Journal of Educational Measurement* 15, 1978, 321-327.

Hambleton, R. K., et al. Criterion-referenced testing and measurement: a review of technical issues and developments. *Review of Educational Research* 48, 1978, 1-47.

Harris, C. W. An interpretation of Livingston's reliability coefficient for criterion-referenced tests. *Journal of Educational Measurement* 9, 1972, 27-30.

Hsu, T. C. Empirical data on criterion-referenced tests. Paper presented at the meeting of the American Educational Research Association, New York, February 1971.

Jackson, R. Developing criterion-referenced tests. T. M. *Reports* No. 15. Princeton, N.J.: Educational Testing Service, 1970.

Kriewall, T. E. Aspects and applications of criterion-referenced tests. Paper presented at the meeting of the American Educational Research Association, Chicago, April 1972.

Livingston, S. A. *The reliability of criterion-referenced measures*. Report No. 73. Baltimore: Center for the Study of Social Organization of the Schools, The Johns Hopkins University, 1970.

_____ . Criterion-referenced applications of classical test theory. *Journal of Educational Measurement* 9, 1972, 13-27.

Morrison, H. C. *The practice of teaching in the secondary school*. Chicago: University of Chicago Press, 1926.

Pittman, J. Actions taken by State Departments of Education in Developing CBTE Certifications Systems. Speech delivered at the ATE National Conference in New Orleans, February 6, 1975.

Popham, W. J. Normative data for criterion-referenced tests? *Phi Delta Kappan* 58, 1976, 593-594.

_____ . As always provocative. *Journal of Educational Measurement* 15, 1978, 297-300.

_____. Indices of adequacy for criterion-referenced test items. Symposium presented at the annual meeting of the American Educational Research Association and the National Council on Measurement in Education, Minneapolis, March 1970.

Popham, W. J., and Husek, T. R.   Implications of criterion-referenced measurement. *Journal of Educational Measurement* 6, 1969, 1-9.

Schmieder, A. A. The last relatively complete tentative bibliography on competency-based education. In W. R. Houston, *Exploring competency-based education.* Berkeley, Calif.: McCutchen, 1974, 367-426.

Smythe, M. J., Kibler, R. J., and Hutchings, P. W. A comparison of norm-referenced and criterion-referenced measurement with implications for communication instruction. *The Speech Teacher* 22, 1973, 1-17.

Thorndike, E. L. The nature, purposes and general methods of measurements of educational products. In G. M. Whipple (Ed.), *The measurement of educational products*, Part II. Seventeenth Yearbook of the National Society for the Study of Education. Bloomington, Ind.: Bloomington Public School Company, 1918.

Washburne, C. W. Educational measurement as a key to individual instruction and promotions. *Journal of Educational Research* 5, 1922, 195-206.

Westbrook, D. C., and Sandefur, W. Involvement of American Association of Colleges for teacher education institutions in CBTE programs. *Phi Delta Kappan* 57, 1975, 276-277.

Wright, A. R., and Doxsey, J. R. *Measurement in support of affective education.* Salt Lake City: Interstate Educational Resource Service Center, 1972.

Zieky, M. J., and Livingston, S. A. *Manual for setting standards on the Basic Skills Assessment Tests.* Princeton, N. J.: Educational Testing Service, 1977.

Samples of Instructional Objectives

An efficient means of learning to write instructional objectives is to observe "models" of objectives that have been written by other teachers and curriculum planners. The purpose of this section is to provide a *variety* of such models encompassing a wide range of subject matter. All of the sample objectives included have been written for actual classroom use and, in many cases, have been published as part of a curriculum guide.

The examples include a broad range of styles and formats. Some of those objectives provided do not follow the format for writing instructional objectives that we have suggested. However, we thought that sample objectives of varying formats would be helpful to teachers in making decisions about the most desirable format to use for their purposes. The sample objectives included are not purported to be examples of "excellence" in the craft of objective formulation—they are included primarily to provide concrete examples of the types of instructional objectives that are currently in use.

PMI Objectives[1]

Given a rectangle that has been divided into a number of equal squares of which some are shaded, the student will be able to specify the fractional part of the rectangle that is shaded. (Pictorial fractions)

Given a number line showing the operation of addition of whole numbers and an appropriate open mathematical sentence, the student will be able to complete the mathematical sentence to describe the operation.

Given an addition problem with two negative integers as addends, the student will be able to supply a missing addend in the commuted form of the problem.

Given a multiplication problem with three positive fractions as factors parenthesized to show a particular grouping of factors, the student will be able to supply a missing factor in the problem parenthesized to show a different grouping of factors.

Given an equation with a missing factor, where the sum is implicit in a mixed number, the student will be able to apply the distributive property in supplying the missing factor.

Given a number less than 10 and a table of numbers such as a section of a hundreds chart, the student will be able to mark all of the multiples of the given number on the chart.

Given an illustration of an acute angle overlayed by a protractor, the student will be able to indicate the measure of the angle in degrees.

Given a drawing of a trapezoid subdivided into a parallelogram and an equilateral triangle with all dimensions shown, the student will be able to compute the area of the figure.

Given a matrix of values for an arbitrary, abstract system under an abstract operation and two equations, the second derived from the first, the student will be able to derive a third equation demonstrating the associative property for the operation. (Abstract systems)

Given a right triangle with the lengths of the sides indicated, the student will be able to specify the sine of one of the acute angles as a fraction.

---

[1] From John Gessel, *Teacher's Guide for Use with the Prescriptive Mathematics Inventory.* Copyright © 1972 by McGraw-Hill, Inc. Reprinted by permission of the publisher, CTB/McGraw-Hill, Del Monte Research Park, Monterey, Calif., 93940. All rights reserved. Printed in the U.S.A.

Educational Psychology[2]

Upon reading the first section of this chapter (on a theory of teaching), you should be able to meet these objectives:

1. Indicate the three questions about teaching behavior that a theory of teaching answers and provide an illustration of a theory of teaching that raises and answers these questions.
2. Point out characteristics (in terms of questions raised and answered) that distinguish a theory of teaching from a theory of learning; describe the relationship between a theory of teaching and a theory of learning; and provide illustrations of a theory of teaching and of a theory of learning that indicate these distinctions and relationships.
3. Point out characteristics (in terms of questions raised and answered) that distinguish a theory of teaching from a philosophy of education; illustrate these distinctions by comparing a teaching theory and a philosophy of education.

Upon reading the second and third sections of this chapter (on models of teaching), you should be able to meet these objectives:

4. List the four components of the basic teaching model and illustrate how a feedback loop from performance assessment results in adjustments in the three remaining components.
5. Describe the psychological teaching models of a) Stolurow, b) Carroll, and c) Flanders in terms of the components of the basic teaching model.
6. Describe the historical teaching models of a) Socrates, b) the Jesuits, and c) Combs and Snygg in terms of the components of the basic teaching model.

Upon reading the first section of this chapter (on the definition of entering behavior), you should be able to meet these objectives:

1. List the major characteristics of entering behavior.
2. Distinguish entering behavior from and relate it to terminal performance by pointing out similar and dissimilar characteristics.

---

[2] From John P. DeCecco, *The Psychology of Learning and Instruction: Educational Psychology,* © 1968. Reprinted by permission of Prentice-Hall, Inc., Englewood Cliffs, N.J., pp. 5 and 6, 57 and 58.

3. Distinguish entering behavior from and relate it to readiness, maturation, individual differences, and personality by pointing out similar and dissimilar characteristics.
4. Illustrate relevant entering behavior for an instructional objective of your own choice.

VAE Systems Project

VAE 5134 Advanced Typewriting[3]

Given a typewriting lesson plan, the student will evaluate it and make the following revisions:

a. develop new supplementary materials for beginning the lesson;
b. develop new consumer and job topics pertinent to the lesson;
c. if necessary, revise directions to ensure clarity and precise communication;
d. if necessary, revise the presentation of content if the facts presented are not accurate;
e. if necessary, construct a closer integration between the component parts of the lesson plan;
f. if necessary, edit the plan to eliminate errors in spelling punctuation, grammar, or syntax;
g. if necessary, make changes so that the plan conforms to the format specified for a typewriting lesson plan.

The student will demonstrate at least five of the following classroom management procedures:

a. attendance procedures;
b. distribution of materials;
c. care of equipment;
d. talking only when it is quiet;
e. chalkboard use;
f. use of instructional equipment;
g. techniques of testing (i.e., handling results, recording test scores).

---

[3] From T. Johnson, R. Richey, and B. Moy, *VAE Pre-Certification Teacher Education Program: Competencies & Performance Objectives*, Series No. 1. Detroit: Wayne State University, 1972, pp. 728–39. Reprinted by permission of the authors.

Criteria for each of the above management skills will be provided. This demonstration will occur during the forty-fifty-minute teaching performance that takes place in actual typing classes in Metropolitan Detroit.

The student will teach one forty-fifty-minute typing lesson to secondary students in the Metropolitan Detroit area. The groups may be either small groups or total typing classes. The lesson for this teaching experience will be:

a. written according to the VAE format incorporating the specified components of a typing lesson plan;
b. either revised lessons dealt with in class or newly developed plans;
c. based upon entry level job skills;
d. incorporated into the sequence of lessons currently being taught by the existing teacher in that classroom;
e. approved by the VAE instructor and the classroom teacher;
f. utilize demonstration and questioning techniques as well as other appropriate delivery systems if possible.

The teaching performance will be evaluated on the following basic teaching skills:

a. beginning a lesson;
b. clarity of presentation;
c. pupil participation and attention;
d. questioning skills;
e. pacing of the lesson;
f. selection and use of supplementary materials, including:
1) the use of transparencies according to the specifications provided
2) thought starters
3) quality of the reproduction of handouts
4) ASA drills;
g. ending lesson.

In addition, this teaching performance task will be evaluated using scores from three-five-minute exit tests or products that measure the lesson's performance objectives. Finally, a statement will be provided from the classroom teacher that the pre-intern has passed the objective.

The student will identify new ideas on how to teach typewriting from at least five articles written within the last five years that deal with classroom experiments or practical experiences. Each article must be summarized using the Turabian annotation format. The five articles must each deal with a different topic from the following areas of instruction:

a. upper alphabetic keys;
b. lower alphabetic keys;
c. home row keys;
d. numeric and special keys;
e. margins;
f. horizontal centering;
g. vertical centering;
h. tabulations;
i. letters and memos;
j. erasing;
k. crowding and spreading;
l. composing at the typewriter.

VAE 5187 Methods and Materials of Instruction I[4]

Using the projected teaching specialization as a basis for content selection and the unit plan format developed in objective #07146, the student will develop a written unit teaching plan that includes a preface describing the specific teaching situation for which the unit plan has been designed. Topic #6 in *Teaching Successfully*, along with student-selected references, should be used as a guide for the development of the unit teaching plan. A project teaching plan may be developed as a unit teaching plan.

Using the example of safety instruction for the engine lathe on pages 408-411 of *Teaching Successfully*, the student will prepare in written outline form the safety instruction for a machine that would be included in the laboratory equipment of the projected teaching specialization.

Using Topic #3 of *Teaching Successfully* and current reference materials, the student will analyze possible learner handi-

---

[4] From G. Harold Silvius and Arthur Deane, *VAE Pre-Certification Teacher Education Program: Competencies and Performance Objectives*, Series No. 1. Detroit: Wayne State University, 1972, pp. 728-57. Reprinted by permission of the authors.

caps that they will probably need to deal with in an industrial education laboratory. These would include consideration for learners who are left-handed or with:

a. defective vision;
b. impaired hearing;
c. a speech defect;
d. a crippled condition;
e. poor mental health.

Using the projected teaching specialization and Topics #9 & #10 of *Teaching Successfully* as a guide, the student will develop written criteria for evaluating text, reference, and visual materials (transparencies, films, etc.) for a specific learning situation. The criteria will be written in standard outline format. The outline of criteria will include a preface briefly describing the learning situation for which the criteria have been developed. The student's ability to analyze a given situation involving student handicaps will be evaluated on the course examination.

Using the projected teaching specialization and the text, *Teaching Successfully*, as a guide, the student will design a *total record-keeping system* that could be adapted to future classroom/laboratory experiences. This record-keeping system should include:

a. class books;
b. individual progress charts;
c. accident reports;
d. safety records;
e. informal pertinent data concerning students;
f. other pertinent records that the student feels are needed to administer the projected teaching specialization.

The format of the record-keeping system will follow the form of a standard written outline. The outline will include a preface that describes the learning situation for which the record-keeping system has been designed.

Self-concept Objectives: Primary Level[5]

Direct Self-Report

Objective No. 1. (Comprehensive) Students will evidence positive self-concepts by indicating agreement with questions that reflect positive perceptions of the self in relation to family, peers, scholastic achievement, and about the self in general; and by indicating disagreement with questions that reflect negative perceptions of self in these areas.

Objective No. 2. (Peer) Students will display positive self-concepts in the peer dimension by indicating agreement with questions that reflect positive peer relations or positive perceptions of the self in social situations; and by indicating disagreement with negative questions.

Objective No. 3. (School) Students will evidence positive self-concepts in the school dimension by expressing agreement with questions concerned with success or perceived esteem in scholastic endeavors; and by indicating disagreement with questions concerned with perceived failure or lack of achievement.

Objective No. 4. (Family) Students will exhibit positive self-concepts in the family dimension by indicating agreement with questions that present positive perceptions of self in terms of family relationships or situations; and by indicating disagreement with negative questions.

Objective No. 5. (General) Students will evidence positive self-concepts about the self in general by expressing agreement with questions that depict a person with positive self-esteem; and by indicating disagreement with questions that depict a person with negative self-esteem.

Inferential Self-Report

Objective No. 6. (General) Students will display positive self-concepts by indicating their *willingness* to play a wide variety of

---

[5] From Instructional Objectives Exchange, *Measures of Self Concept: K-12*, rev. ed. Los Angeles: Instructional Objectives Exchange, 1972, pp. 19–21 and 26–28. Reprinted by permission of the Instructional Objectives Exchange.

roles in an imaginary television show, when given the opportunity to select an unlimited number of parts that they would play.

Objective No. 7. (Peer) Students will display positive self-concepts by indicating that others would choose them to play roles that carry positive images in a pretend play.

Objective No. 8. (Family) Students will display positive self-concepts by selecting responses that indicate that their mothers would not dislike them if they engaged in actions usually expected to yield parental disapproval.

Observational Indicators

Objective No. 9. When given the opportunity to display classwork, students will give evidence of positive self-concepts by voluntarily posting their work.

Objective No. 10. Given a contrived situation in which the teacher describes a group of fictitiously esteemed students, class members will demonstrate positive self-concepts by voluntarily identifying themselves as students who belong to this group.

Objectives for Attitudes Related to Tolerance: Grade 9-12[6]

Objective 1: Students will indicate agreement with statements indicative of a tolerant attitude toward others, and disagreement with statements indicative of an intolerant attitude toward others. *Tolerance* is here considered to be the willingness not to interfere with the activities of others and the rejection of cultural stereotypes.

Objective 2: Students will indicate agreement with statements indicative of a desire to seek out unfamiliar social and cultural situations, and disagreement with statements indicative of a rejection of such experiences.

Objective 3: Students will indicate acceptance of a variety of policy statements that have been judged to express tolerance of the values and opinions of others, and opposition to statements judged to reflect intolerant policies.

---

[6] From Instructional Objectives Exchange, *Attitudes Related to Tolerance: Grades 9-12.* Los Angeles: Instructional Objectives Exchange, 1971, pp. 13–16. Reprinted by permission of the Instructional Objectives Exchange.

Objective 4: Students will indicate disagreement with statements tending to stereotype beliefs and behavior of people within cultural groups, and agreement with statements suggesting that individuals vary significantly within such groups.

Objective 5: Given hypothetical situations concerning a generalized other and alternative reactions, the student will select the reactions indicative of a desire or willingness to associate with people of different racial groups, to see people of different racial groups in favorable status situations, and to see them as dominant or successful. In cases of illegal or detrimental behavior the student will select reactions indicative of a rejection of such behavior.

Objective 6: Given hypothetical situations and alterative reactions, the student will select the reactions indicative of tolerance toward certain behavior and personal beliefs of people of given races. *Tolerance* as measured here is defined as the willingness not to interfere in the beliefs or activities of others.

Objective 7: Given a list of positive and negative statements about specific races, the student will reflect positive attitudes by selecting the alternative "very many" in response to how many of the people possess each positive characteristic and "very few" in response to how many possess each negative characteristic.

Objective 8: Students will, when given a series of hypothetical situations and alternative solutions, select the solutions that have been judged to reflect a tolerant attitude toward the values and opinions of others.

Objective 9: Given a series of hypothetical situations concerning specific races or other people in general and alternative reactions, the student will select the responses that reflect a tolerant attitude.

Sample Instructional Objectives for the Language Arts[7]

Given a set of kernel sentences with an adjective and a predicate, the student will identify the adjective and the predicate.

Given a group of incomplete sentences requiring adjectives, the student will supply adjectives to complete the sentences.

---

[7] From Instructional Objectives Exchange, *Language Arts 4-6.* Los Angeles: Center for the Study of Evaluation, UCLA Graduate School of Education, 1966. Reprinted by permission of the Instructional Objectives Exchange.

Given incomplete sentences that include a choice of pronouns in different cases, the student will select the pronoun in the correct form to complete each sentence.

Given a set of compound sentences, the student will 1) identify the independent clauses in each sentence and 2) identify the conjunction that connects them.

Given orally a list of spelling words containing three-letter blends, the students will 1) spell the words correctly; 2) underline the blends; and 3) organize the words by rewriting them into appropriate grouping under one of the following labels: *str, thr, squ, spl, scr, spr.*

Given kernel sentences with a blank space in the subject and/or object position, the student will select and write the correct personal pronoun to complete each sentence.

Given a list of singular nouns and a set of rules for forming noun plurals, the student will select the appropriate rule for forming the noun plural for each of the singular nouns, write the correct plural for that noun, and write the numerical representation of the rule for plural formation that governs each noun.

Given a list of base nouns, the student will: 1) in one column add the morpheme *ful* to each base noun; 2) in a second column write each word thus created with stress marks to demonstrate the pronunciation; and 3) in a third column indicate whether each newly formed word is a noun or an adjective according to its stress pattern. The *adjective* has the stress pattern, "first-weak"; the *noun* has the stress pattern, "first-second."

Given the rules for capitalization and a set of twelve sentences that contain no capitalization, the student will rewrite each sentence using the appropriate capitalization and identify the rule for each change by writing the rule after the sentence.

Given a set of rules for the use of the colon and a set of sentences that require insertion of colons, the student will place each colon properly and identify the rule appropriate to each placement.

Given an oral conversation through dictation, the student will record the conversation in written form, observing and using established paragraph form and supplying in the appropriate places quotation marks, capital letters, and terminal punctuation.

Given an assignment to write a three-paragraph theme about three separate but related objects, the student will demonstrate his understanding of proper paragraphing by writing about each of the objects in a separate paragraph. The paragraphs will conform to prespecified criteria. *Paragraph form* is defined as an indented first line and *paragraph unity* is defined as all sentences pertaining to the topic idea.

The student will write a fictional story about a particular country based upon factual information taken from the encyclopedia. The story should have a main character and should include action or details that are both consistent with the country described and representative of that country.

Given an assignment to develop a story plot, the student will write a story incorporating the following criteria:

1. He will include at least two characters, with the main character involved in a challenge or a struggle.
2. He will include a climax to the story that results from the presentation of details in a sequential order.
3. He will include a climax that is determined by and prepared for by the events of the story.

Program Text Designed to Teach Students How to Use Instructional Objectives

Our experiences in using instructional objectives suggest that students learn more efficiently and effectively when they first are taught how to use instructional objectives. The programmed text contained in this section is intended to be general in terms of the subject matter and evaluation procedures used with objectives, but specific to the instructional objective format presented in Chapter 2. The teacher may be required to modify the program to suit one's own particular style of objective writing, content, and/or evaluation procedures. The program is designed to serve as an example. We encourage you either to use the program in its current form or to develop one for your particular needs.

Introduction

The following program is designed to teach you how to use instructional objectives. If this program is successful, after completing it, you should be able to:

1. State the five components of instructional objectives;

2. Identify the five components of instructional objectives given to you by your teacher;
3. Use instructional objectives to prepare for tests and to study more effectively.

1

Instructional objectives are statements that describe what students will be able to do after completing a prescribed unit of instruction. For example, an instructional objective for a unit in history might be: "Given thirty minutes, the student will be able to list in writing three major factors that gave rise to the Industrial Revolution."

Instructional objectives are important to you as a student because they inform you:
1. What information is important to learn.
2. How you will be asked to demonstrate that you have learned the required material.

Go to the Next Frame

2

Instructional objectives are _____

_____ .

They are important to students because _____ .

1.

2.

Go to the Next Frame

3

Your responses to the preceding frame should have been: *Instructional objectives are statements that describe what students will be able to do after completing a prescribed unit of instruction.* They are important to you as students because *they inform you:*
1. *What information is important to learn.*
2. *How you will be asked to demonstrate that you have learned the required material.*

Go to the Next Frame

—————————————————————————————————— 4

While the particular format of instructional objectives may vary from teacher to teacher, all good instructional objectives have in common components informing students what is to be learned and how learning is to be demonstrated.

In this program we will examine five components of instructional objectives:

1. *Who* is to perform the desired behavior (e.g., "the student").
2. The *actual behavior* to be employed in demonstrating mastery of the objective (e.g., "to write," "to speak").
3. The *result* (i.e., the product or performance) of the behavior, which will be evaluated to determine whether the objective is mastered (e.g., "an essay" or "the term paper").
4. The *relevant conditions* under which the behavior is to be performed (e.g., "in a one-hour quiz" or "in front of the class")
5. The *standard* that will be used to evaluate the success of the product or performance (e.g., "90 percent correct" or "four out of five correct").

Go to the Next Frame

—————————————————————————————————— 5

The five components of instructional objectives are:

1. _____
2. _____
3. _____
4. _____
5. _____

Go to the Next Frame

—————————————————————————————————— 6

Your response to Frame 5 should look something like this:

1. Who is to perform the desired behavior (e.g., "the student").

2. The actual behavior to be employed in demonstrating mastery of the objective (e.g., "to write," "to speak").
3. The result (i.e., the product or performance) of the behavior, which will be evaluated to determine whether the objective is mastered (e.g., "an essay" or "the term paper").
4. The relevant conditions under which the behavior is to be performed (e.g., "in a one-hour quiz" or "in front of the class").
5. The standard that will be used to evaluate the success of the product or performance (e.g., "90 percent correct" or "four out of five correct").

Go to the Next Frame

7

Here are five components of instructional objectives:

1. Who is to perform the desired behavior.
2. The actual behavior to be employed in demonstrating mastery of the objectives.
3. The result (i.e., product or performance) of the behavior, which will be evaluated to determine whether the objective is mastered.
4. The relevant conditions under which the behavior is to be performed.
5. The standard that will be used to evaluate the success of the product or performance.

Examine the following objective, and see if you can identify the five components of instructional objectives (underline each component and place the number—i.e., 1-5—of the component above that which corresponds to the portion of the objective you have underlined).

Given a list of twenty pairs of chemical compounds and/or elements, the student will provide in writing complete chemical reactions for 80 percent of the pairs using the standard symbols as indicated in the textbook.

Go to the Next Frame

⑧

Your response should look like this:

4
Given a list of twenty pairs of chemical com-

1   2
pounds and/or elements, the student will provide

3
in writing complete chemical reactions for 80

5
percent of the pairs using the standard symbols

as indicated in the textbook.

1. Who is to perform the desired behavior.
2. The actual behavior to be employed in demonstrating mastery of the objectives.
3. The result (i.e., product or performance) of the behavior, which will be evaluated to determine whether the objective is mastered.
4. The relevant conditions under which the behavior is to be performed.
5. The standard that will be used to evaluate the success of the product or performance.

Well, how did you do? If you were unable to identify all of the five components, don't worry.

Go to the Next Frame

⑨

There should be little or no problem in identifying the first component of instructional objectives (i.e., who is to perform the behavior), since it will always be YOU— the student. However, you probably will encounter a variety of actual behaviors, results, relevant conditions, and standards in objectives that teachers present to you. To help you use instructional objectives most efficiently, let us examine each of these components more closely to see exactly what information you should obtain from each component.

Go to the Next Frame

10

As you know, the second component of instructional objectives informs students of the *actual behavior* to be employed in demonstrating mastery of the objective. Examples of typical "action verbs" used by teachers to communicate this message to students are listed below:

1. identifying
2. distinguishing
3. constructing
4. naming
5. ordering
6. describing
7. stating a rule
8. applying a role
9. demonstrating
10. interpreting

Go to the Next Frame

11

It is important that you become sensitive to the type of information provided for you by the second component (i.e., actual behavior) of instructional objectives. Consider the following objectives. Rank the objectives from 1-3 on the relative difficulty of the behavior required to demonstrate mastery of each objective [using 1 as being the most difficult].

1. Given twenty math problems, the student will apply the distributive law in solving at least eighteen problems correctly.
2. Given twenty minutes, the student will list in the correct order the steps a bill must go through before becoming a law.
3. Given twenty minutes, the student will write an essay comparing and contrasting at least three types of government.

Go to the Next Frame

12

We would rank the objectives as follows. How do your rankings compare? If they are the same as below, go to Frame 14; if not, go to Frame 13.

1. Given twenty minutes, the student will write an essay comparing and contrasting at least three types of government.

2. Given twenty math problems, the student will apply the distributive law in solving at least eighteen problems correctly.
3. Given twenty minutes, the student will list in the correct order the steps a bill must go through before becoming a law.

— 13

Look at the three objectives again:

1. Given twenty minutes, the student will write an essay comparing and contrasting at least three types of government.
2. Given twenty math problems, the student will apply the distributive law in solving at least eighteen problems correctly.
3. Given twenty minutes, the student will list in the correct order the steps a bill must go through before becoming a law.

Note that the first objective indicates that you will be expected "to write an essay comparing and contrasting. . . ." In our estimation, this would appear more difficult than merely listing steps in the correct order or applying the same rule to several problems. Writing an essay would involve organizing and expressing thoughts clearly in addition to demonstrating knowledge about the topic of the essay.

Similarly, applying a rule in solving math problems would appear more difficult than merely listing steps in the correct order. One could simply memorize the steps in correct order, but one cannot memorize how to apply a math rule to unique problems.

One method for utilizing the information provided by the second component of instructional objectives is to ask yourself: 1) exactly what is it that you are required to *do*, and 2) how would you study most efficiently to enable you to perform the required behavior.

Go to the Next Frame

— 14

The third component of instructional objectives indicates the product or performance that will be evaluated by the teacher. This component is particularly important because it often conveys specific information about what is to be studied. For example, consider the objectives below; underline the part of each objective that conveys information about the product or performance that is to be evaluated:

1. Given twenty minutes, the student will correctly translate at least twenty out of twenty-five Spanish words into their English equivalents.
2. Given ten minutes, the student will draw a model of communication and label each component in the model.
3. Given a bar graph of production rate, the student will write an essay comparing and contrasting the rate of production over a five-year period.

Go to the Next Frame

15

Your responses should look something like this:

1. Given twenty minutes, the student will correctly translate at least twenty out of twenty-five <u>Spanish words into their English equivalents.</u>
2. Given ten minutes, the student will draw a <u>model of communication</u> and label <u>each component in the model.</u>
3. Given a bar graph of production rate, the student will write <u>an essay comparing and contrasting the rate of production over a five-year period.</u>

If your responses match with ours, go to Frame 17; if not, go to Frame 16.

16

Examine the objectives again:

1. Given twenty minutes, the student will correctly translate at least twenty out of twenty-five Spanish words into their English equivalents.
2. Given ten minutes, the student will draw a model of communication and label each component in the model.

3. Given a bar graph of production rate, the student will write an essay comparing and contrasting the rate of production over a five-year period.

Note that in the first objective the result of the student behavior (i.e., translating) is a list of *Spanish words with their English equivalents.* The result of the student behavior always is the product or performance—that is, the third component of instructional objectives.

Similarly, the result of drawing in the second objective is *a model of communication* with *each component labeled.* In the third objective the result of comparing and contrasting is *an essay on the rate of production over a five-year period.*

Got it?!!

Go to the Next Frame

17

The fourth component of instructional objectives indicates the conditions under which the required behavior is to be performed: for example, how much time you will be given; whether you will be given any reference materials, etc. It is sometimes difficult for a teacher to include all of the conditions under which a given behavior will be performed. However, good objectives contain at least the most essential information regarding the conditions under which the behavior is to be demonstrated. For example:

1. When presented with a typed list . . .
2. Given a slide rule and twenty minutes . . .
3. Without any reference materials or notes . . .
4. Given a tape recording . . .
5. Given a reference book . . .

Go to the Next Frame

18

Individuals sometimes confuse the fourth and fifth components of instructional objectives. We already know that the fourth component conveys information about the relevant conditions under which the behavior will be demonstrated. But what was that fifth component?

Go to the Next Frame

19

The fifth component of instructional objectives is *the standard (or criterion) that will be used to evaluate your performance.*

Certainly this is an important bit of information for a student to know. The standard indicates what a correct response is and how correct a response must be before it is considered acceptable. Examine the following objective and underline the part indicating the standard of evaluation.

Given one hour and no reference materials, the student will write an essay synthesizing the causes and consequences of World War II. The essay must contain at least three of the major causes and three of the major consequences that were discussed in the textbook.

Go to the Next Frame

20

Your response should look like this:

Given one hour and no reference materials, the student will write an essay synthesizing the causes and consequences of World War II. The essay must contain at least three of the major causes and three of the major consequences that were discussed in the textbook.

How did you do? Try to identify the standard in these objectives:

1. Given a list of twenty unpunctuated sentences, the student will rewrite each sentence and correctly punctuate at least eighteen of the twenty sentences.

2. Given 100 words presented orally, the student will spell correctly at least 85 percent of the words.
3. Given a 100-word business letter, the student will type the letter within 1½ minutes and make no errors.

Go to the Next Frame

21

Your response should look like this:

1. Given a list of twenty unpunctuated sentences, the student will rewrite each sentence and correctly punctuate at least eighteen of the twenty sentences.
2. Given 100 words presented orally, the student will spell correctly at least 85 percent of the words.
3. Given a 100-word business letter, the student will type the letter within 1½ minutes and make no errors.

Go to the Next Frame

22

At this point you should be reasonably familiar with the five components of instructional objectives and what kind of information each component provides you.

You should keep in mind that teachers often have different ways of stating objectives, so you may not always find all of the components we have discussed. However, all good instructional objectives will inform you: 1) what information is important to learn and 2) how you will be asked to demonstrate that you have learned the required material.

Go to the Next Frame

23

In summary, describe what information is conveyed by the following objective:

Given a diagram of an internal combustion engine and one hour, the student will label at least 80 percent of the components of the diagram and describe how they function.

_____

_____

_____

_____

Go to the Next Frame

24

While the wording may differ, your response should indicate the following points:

1. That you will be provided with a diagram of an internal combustion engine.
2. That you will be given an hour to produce the required product.
3. That the product consists of a diagram with labeled components and a description of how each component functions.
4. That at least 80 percent of the components in the diagram must be labeled and described before the answer is acceptable.

THE END

Instrumentation of Bloom's and Krathwohl's Taxonomies for the Writing of Educational Objectives[1]

During the past six or eight years an increased amount of attention has been given to the statement of educational objectives in behavioral terms both to facilitate the evaluation of educational programs and to improve the validity of the measures and scales utilized in the evaluation process (Metfessel and Michael, 1967; Michael and Metfessel, 1966). Although set up as a programmed learning text, Mager's (1962) *Preparing Instructional Objectives* has been one of the most useful guides to teachers and specialists in curriculum who have sought help in stating the desired outcomes of instruction in behavioral language—in describing the kinds of specific and relatively terminal behaviors that the learner will be capable of exhibiting subsequent to exposure to a program of instruction. Another useful source has been the volume edited by Lindvall (1964) who, in collaboration with Nardozza and Felton (Lindvall, Nardozza, and Felton, 1964) not only prepared a chapter concerned with the importance of specific objectives in curric-

[1] Newton S. Metfessel, W. B. Michael, and D. A. Kirsner, "Instrumentation of Bloom's and Krathwohl's Taxonomies for the Writing of Educational Objectives," *Psychology in the Schools* 6, No. 3, July 1969, 227–231. Reprinted by permission.

ular development, but also enlisted the aid of several distinguished educators, e.g., Krathwohl (1964) and Tyler (1964) with specialized interests in evaluation. Such efforts have essentially involved a fusion of curriculum design with the evaluation process in that curricular planning is described in terms of behavioral objectives that are necessary for the construction of valid tests and scales. The taxonomies provide the required model necessary to furnish meaningful evidence regarding the attainment of desired behavioral changes.

Although Krathwohl (1964) related the taxonomy of educational objectives in both the cognitive (Bloom, 1956) and the affective (Krathwohl, Bloom, and Masia, 1964) domains to curriculum building, he was able to present only a limited number of concrete illustrations, some of which Mager would probably challenge because of their relative lack of specificity. Admittedly, Krathwohl has made an important and helpful start in relating objectives to a meaningful and rather well-known conceptual framework. However, the writers believe that there exists a need for an instrumentation of the taxonomy of educational objectives within both the cognitive and affective domains—that is, a more clear-cut description of how the taxonomy can be implemented in the school setting. The approach utilized was the development of *behaviorally-oriented* infinitives which, when combined with given objects, would form a basis for meaningful, cohesive, and operational statements.

Purpose

Thus the essential purpose of this paper was to show how specific behavioral objectives can be formulated within the hierarchy of the major levels and sublevels of the taxonomies of educational objectives as set forth by Bloom (1956) and Krathwohl (1964). Such a framework should furnish a helpful base around which behavioral statements of objectives can be formulated.

Definition

An educational objective consists of a description of the behaviors of an individual (the learner or examinee) in relation to processing of information embodied in subject matter—that is, what the learner must be capable of doing with certain characteristics or properties of subject matter. The behavioral component, which may be described as a process involved at an appropriate level of the taxonomic classification, is usually expressed in the form of a noun "ability" or a verb of being "able" followed by an infinitive such as the "ability to do" or "able to do." The second component of the objective, which consists of the specific content often found in the formal learning experience (e.g., in the curricular or instructional unit), constitutes a direct object of the verb or infinitive form. The terms "subject matter" or "content" are used in a fairly broad sense, as their level of specificity is highly variable, depending upon the characteristics of the curricular unit.

Instrumentation

To facilitate the formulation of statements of specific behavioral objectives within the framework of Bloom's taxonomy, the writers have included a table made up of three columns. The first column contains the taxonomic classification identified by both code number and terminology employed in Bloom's (1956) taxonomy. The entries in the second column consist of appropriate infinitives that the teacher or curriculum worker may consult in order to achieve a precise or preferred wording of the behavior or activity desired. In the third column somewhat general terms relative to subject matter properties are stated. These direct objects, which may be expanded upon to furnish specificity at a desired level, may be permuted with one or more of the infinitive forms to yield the basic structure of an educational objective—activity (process) followed by content (subject matter property). At the discretion of the reader the words "ability" or "able" can be inserted in front of each of the infinitives.

    Although within a given major process level or sublevel of the taxonomy each infinitive cannot in all instances be meaningfully or idiomatically paired with every direct object listed, many useful permutations of infinitives and direct objects that furnish entirely readable statements are possible. Certainly use of these tables should lead to a substantial gain in the clarity

TABLE I.   Instrumentation of the Taxonomy of
Educational Objectives: Cognitive Domain

| | KEY WORDS | |
Taxonomy Classification	Examples of Infinitives	Examples of Direct Objects
1.00 Knowledge		
1.10 Knowledge of Specifics		
1.11 Knowledge of Terminology	to define, to distinguish, to acquire, to identify, to recall, to recognize	vocabulary, terms, terminology, meaning(s), definitions, referents, elements
1.12 Knowledge of Specific Facts	to recall, to recognize, to acquire, to identify	facts, factual information, (sources), (names), (dates), (events), (persons), (places), (time periods), properties, examples, phenomena
1.20 Knowledge of Ways and Means of Dealing with Specifics		
1.21 Knowledge of Conventions	to recall, to identify, to recognize, to acquire	form(s), conventions, uses, usage, rules, ways, devices, symbols, representations, style(s), format(s)
1.22 Knowledge of Trends and Sequences	to recall, to recognize, to acquire, to identify	action(s), processes, movement(s), continuity, development(s), trend(s), sequence(s), causes, relationship(s), forces, influences
1.23 Knowledge of Classifications and Categories	to recall, to recognize, to acquire, to identify	area(s), type(s), feature(s), class(es), set(s), division(s), arrangement(s), classification(s), category/ categories
1.24 Knowledge of Criteria	to recall, to recognize, to acquire, to identify	criteria, basics, elements
1.25 Knowledge of Methodology	to recall, to recognize, to acquire, to identify	methods, techniques, approaches, uses, procedures, treatments

TABLE I (Continued)

| Taxonomy Classification | KEY WORDS | |
	Examples of Infinitives	Examples of Direct Objects
1.30 Knowledge of the Universals and Abstractions in a Field		
1.31 Knowledge of Principles and Generalizations	to recall, to recognize, to acquire, to identify	principle(s), generalization(s), proposition(s), fundamentals, laws, principal elements, implication(s)
1.32 Knowledge of Theories and Structures	to recall, to recognize, to acquire, to identify	theories, bases, interrelations, structure(s), organization(s), formulation(s)
2.00 Comprehension		
2.10 Translation	to translate, to transform, to give in own words, to illustrate, to prepare, to read, to represent, to change, to rephrase, to restate	meaning(s), sample(s), definitions, abstractions, representations, words, phrases
2.20 Interpretation	to interpret, to reorder, to rearrange, to differentiate, to distinguish, to make, to draw, to explain, to demonstrate	relevancies, relationships, essentials, aspects, new view(s), qualifications, conclusions, methods, theories, abstractions
2.30 Extrapolation	to estimate, to infer, to conclude, to predict, to differentiate, to determine, to extend, to interpolate, to extrapolate, to fill in, to draw	consequences, implications, conclusions, factors, ramifications, meanings, corollaries, effects, probabilities
3.00 Application	to apply, to generalize, to relate, to choose, to develop, to organize, to use, to employ, to transfer, to restructure, to classify	principles, laws, conclusions, effects, methods, theories, abstractions, situations, generalizations, processes, phenomena, procedures
4.00 Analysis		

TABLE I (Continued)

| | KEY WORDS | |
Taxonomy Classification	Examples of Infinitives	Examples of Direct Objects
4.10 Analysis of Elements	to distinguish, to detect, to identify, to classify, to discriminate, to recognize, to categorize, to deduce	elements, hypothesis/ hypotheses, conclusions, assumptions, statements (of fact), statements (of intent), arguments, particulars
4.20 Analysis of Relationships	to analyze, to contrast, to compare, to distinguish, to deduce	relationships, interrelations, relevance, relevancies, themes, evidence, fallacies, arguments, cause-effect(s), consistency/ consistencies, parts, ideas, assumptions
4.30 Analysis of Organizational Principles	to analyze, to distinguish, to detect, to deduce	form(s), pattern(s), purpose(s), point(s) of view(s), techniques, bias(es), structure(s), theme(s), arrangement(s), organization(s)
5.00 Synthesis		
5.10 Production of a Unique Communication	to write, to tell, to relate, to produce, to constitute, to transmit, to originate, to modify, to document	structure(s), pattern(s), product(s), performance(s), design(s), work(s), communications, effort(s), specifics, composition(s)
5.20 Production of a Plan or Proposed Set of Operations	to propose, to plan, to produce, to design, to modify, to specify	plan(s), objectives, specification(s), schematic(s), operations, way(s), solution(s), means
5.30 Derivation of a Set of Abstract Relations	to produce, to derive, to develop, to combine, to organize, to synthesize, to classify, to deduce, to develop, to formulate, to modify	phenomena, taxonomies, concept(s), scheme(s), theories, relationships, abstractions, generalizations, hypothesis/hypotheses, perceptions, ways, discoveries

TABLE I   (Continued)

Taxonomy Classification	KEY WORDS Examples of Infinitives	Examples of Direct Objects
6.00 Evaluation		
6.10 Judgments in Terms of Internal Evidence	to judge, to argue, to validate, to assess, to decide	accuracy/accuracies, consistency/consistencies, fallacies, reliability, flaws, errors, precision, exactness
6.20 Judgments in Terms of External Criteria	to judge, to argue, to consider, to compare, to contrast, to standardize, to appraise	ends, means, efficiency, economy/economies, utility, alternatives, courses of action, standards, theories, generalizations

and speed with which teachers and curriculum specialists, as well as those involved in construction of achievement tests, may state curricular objectives. The writers have found that these tables have been of considerable help to their students, as well as to personnel in public schools who are concerned with writing objectives prior to curriculum development, constructing test items, or carrying out evaluation studies. Slight modifications can be made with the entries to meet the requirements of specific learning situations.

Instrumentation: Affective Domain

The instrumentation of the Affective Domain is the same as that of the Cognitive Domain; to wit, the selection of behaviorally oriented infinitives combined with selected direct objects. As in the case of the Cognitive Domain, these are to be conceptualized as examples for the stimulation of other infinitives and objects and, more important, meaningful objectives in a total framework.

TABLE II.   Instrumentation of the Taxonomy of
Educational Objectives: Affective Domain

| | | KEY WORDS | |
Taxonomy Classification	Examples of Infinitives	Examples of Direct Objects
1.0 Receiving		
1.1 Awareness	to differentiate, to separate, to set apart, to share	sights, sounds, events, designs, arrangements
1.2 Willingness to Receive	to accumulate, to select, to combine, to accept	models, examples, shapes, sizes, meters, cadences
1.3 Controlled or Selected Attention	to select, to posturally respond to, to listen (for), to control	alternatives, answers, rhythms, nuances
2.0 Responding		
2.1 Acquiescence in Responding	to comply (with), to follow, to commend, to approve	directions, instructions, laws, policies, demonstrations
2.2 Willingness to Respond	to volunteer, to discuss, to practice, to play	instruments, games, dramatic works, charades, burlesques
2.3 Satisfaction in Response	to applaud, to acclaim, to spend leisure time in, to augment	speeches, plays, presentations, writings
3.0 Valuing		
3.1 Acceptance of a Value	to increase measured proficiency in, to increase numbers of, to relinquish, to specify	group membership(s), artistic production(s), musical productions, personal friendships
3.2 Preference for a Value	to assist, to subsidize, to help, to support	artists, projects, viewpoints, arguments
3.3 Commitment	to deny, to protest, to debate, to argue	deceptions, irrelevancies, abdications, irrationalities
4.0 Organization		
4.1 Conceptualization of a Value	to discuss, to theorize (on), to abstract, to compare	parameters, codes, standards, goals

TABLE II   (Continued)

| | | KEY WORDS | |
Taxonomy Classification	*Examples of* *Infinitives*	*Examples of* *Direct Objects*
4.2 Organization of A Value System	to balance, to organize, to define, to formulate	systems, approaches, criteria, limits
5.0 Characterization by Value or Value Complex		
5.1 Generalized Set	to revise, to change, to complete, to require	plans, behavior, methods, effort(s)
5.2 Characterization	to be rated high by peers in, to be rated high by superiors in, to be rated high by subordinates in	humanitarianism, ethics, integrity, maturity
	and	
	to avoid, to manage, to resolve, to resist	extravagance(s), ex- cesses, conflicts, exorbitancy/ exorbitancies

Sources for Instructional Objectives: National Clearinghouses and Needs Assessment Materials

While we encourage teachers at all levels of education (i.e., elementary, secondary, and higher) to prepare and use instructional objectives, we recognize that teachers often are too burdened by the demands of their day-to-day job of education to embark on the difficult, time-consuming task of personally constructing instructional objectives and related evaluation measures. Fortunately, other educators have recognized this potential problem and have organized national clearinghouses that make available instructional objectives and corresponding evaluation measures to teachers in several different subject areas. Following is a list of these national clearinghouses to which interested teachers may write and obtain information about the availability of instructional materials relevant to their particular subject areas. We strongly encourage all teachers concerned with instruction to support these clearinghouses by *contributing* their instructional objectives and evaluation measures and by *withdrawing* objectives and test items that are suitable for their particular instructional situation.

OBJECTIVES	*SOURCE*
All subject areas	Instructional Objectives Exchange P.O. Box 24095 Los Angeles, California 90024
All subject areas	*UNIPAC Objectives* Institute for the Development of Educational Advancement (IDEA) University of California Suite 950 1100 Glendon Avenue Los Angeles, California 90024
All subject areas	*Fort Lincoln New Town Objectives (FLINT)* General Learning Corporation 5454 Wisconsin Avenue, NW Washington, D.C. 20015
Special purpose objectives	*Nova Objectives* Mr. Warren Smith Nova High School 36 Southwest 70th Avenue Fort Lauderdale, Florida 33313
Math, Science, Reading	*IPI Objectives* Dr. Robert Scanlon 1700 Market Street Philadelphia, Pennsylvania 19103
Math	*PRIMES Objectives* Doris Cresswell Educational Research Associates Bureau of General and Academic Education Department of Education Box 911 Harrisburg, Pennsylvania 17126
Math	*Clark County Objectives* Clark County School District 2832 East Flamingo Road Las Vegas, Nevada 89109
Math	*Individualized Mathematics System Objectives (IMS)* Mr. Edwar Bruchak Regional Education Lab for the Carolinas & Virginia 613 Vickers Durham, North Carolina 27701

OBJECTIVES	SOURCE
Math, Science, & Specific Reading (not yet available)	*LRA Objectives* Learning Research Associates 1501 Broadway New York, New York 10036
All subject areas	*Directory of Sources of Measurement Objectives* Dr. John Ahlenius Consultant Assessment and Evaluation State Office Building Denver, Colorado 80203

Since needs assessment is an expensive, time-consuming technique that requires expert supervision, many schools do not have the personnel or facilities to conduct accurate needs assessment. The following list of survey and instrument addresses is included to aid you in selecting appropriate kits, models, and instruments for your classroom, school, district, or region.

Consulting Services Corporation
Advisory Council
Seattle, Washington

F. W. English and R. A. Kaufman
Association for Supervision and Curriculum Development
Washington, D. C.

R. M. Gagné
Center for Educational Technology and the College of Education
Florida State University and the Leon County School District
Tallahassee, Florida

M. Hershkowitz
Hershkowitz Associates
Silver Spring, Maryland

B. A. Kaplan
Department of Education
Bureau of Planning
Trenton, New Jersey

R. A. Kaufman and F. W. English
American Association of School Administrators
Washington, D.C.

KOCE-TV
Corporation for Public Broadcasting
Coast Community College District and Washington, D.C.
Costa Mesa, California

T. McCollough, O. W. Markley, and M. Moser
Santa Clara County Component
Office of the Santa Clara County Superintendent of Schools
San Jose, California

Opinion Research Corporation
State Department of Education
Trenton, New Jersey

Office of Planning
South Carolina State Department of Education
Columbia, South Carolina

J. A. Pyatte, M. R. Knight, W. F. Breivogel, and E. P. Durall
Florida Educational Research and Development Council
Gainesville, Florida

J. R. Rowell, Jr.
Center for Community Needs Assessment
University of Florida
Gainesville, Florida

K. D. Tucher
Center for Community Needs Assessment
University of Florida
Gainesville, Florida

B. R. Witkin
National Institute of Education
Alameda County School Department
Hayward, California

B. R. Witkin and K. G. Stephens
Alameda County School Department
Hayward, California

Index